GOD'S AMATEUR

GOD'S AMATEUR

THE WRITING OF
E.C. LARGE

Edited by Stuart Bailey and Robin Kinross

Hyphen Press . London

Published by Hyphen Press, London, in 2008

The book was designed by Stuart Bailey, New York, and typeset & made
into pages by him in Adobe InDesign. The text was output in the typeface
Monotype Gill Sans. Pages were read in proof by Jane Howard, London.
The book was made and printed in Belgium by Die Keure, Bruges.

ISBN 978-0-907259-38-1

www.hyphenpress.co.uk

This book, and the whole project of republishing E.C. Large, would not have
been possible without the wonderful help and support of his daughter and
executor, Jo Major. We are very grateful to her. Thanks also to Norman Potter,
who urged us to read Large.

CONTENTS

I travel now as I have never travelled before: with the knowledge that if I choose this writing will be published. Perhaps that is a good thing to know, perhaps it is not, I am by no means cocksure. I have grown so used to talking to the air, or to myself, with the chance or the hope of publication safely distant, that I fear the nearer presence of the public may cramp my style. I shall begin 'communicating' if I am not very careful. I spoke to an experienced friend of mine about this the other day and he said 'God knows you for an amateur but Fleet Street will call you a pro.' I do not much care what Fleet Street calls me, so long as it helps the sale of my novels, but I rather hope that 'God' will have no reason to change his mind.

E.C. Large, from an unpublished manuscript, 1938 (see p. 55)

(Amateur – one who loves.)

Norman Potter, *What is a designer*, Hyphen Press, 1980

ECL

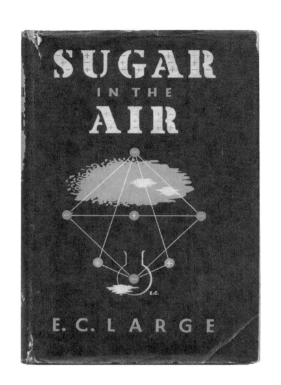
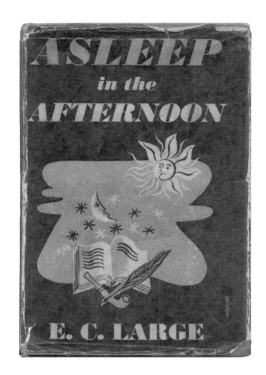
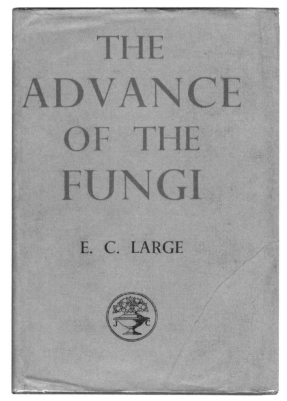

Dust jackets of the first British editions of ECL's four books.

E.C. Large in print

Why republish two novels that have remained out-of-print, almost undisturbed by critics and commentators, for seventy years? The materials that we reprint or publish for the first time in *God's amateur* might seem to compound this odd step; but we believe that they strengthen the case for reissuing the novels.

It was Norman Potter, Hyphen Press's first author, who recommended Large and, in particular, *Sugar in the air*: 'The modern movement has (rightly) been accused of political naïvety by supposing that optimized design was conceivable in mass production, where marketing arrangements will ensure a good product being swept away to stimulate fresh demand. Anyone who wishes to see such matters imaginatively explored should read E.C. Large's novel *Sugar in the air*.' And in a note on this reference he wrote: 'seriously due for a reprint – there is nothing of the kind so well made.'[1]

Sugar in the air can certainly be recommended to designers as showing vividly how it actually is: how design-and-making-and-marketing happens, amid all the contingencies and absurdities of life. But, like any worthwhile creation, the book has other dimensions. And especially when *Asleep in the afternoon*, its sequel, is placed next to it, we then have a two-part work whose complications and reverberations Stuart Bailey discusses in his essay here.

In *God's amateur* we give a substantial taste of Large's contributions as a writer, and at least hint at his contributions as a scientist and also scientific draughtsman. From a surprisingly extensive list of published articles we have selected to show the width of his interests and his methods. By including the pages of typescript (unpublished work) we also give a glimpse of the archive of his work, as well as his skill with the typewriter.

Large quite evidently loved to write. His first substantial published piece appeared in 1930, when he was 28, but it's clear that before then he had given much time and energy to the activity. He began – and resumed, in his retirement – as an amateur writer: amateur in the very best sense. But for a short and intense period (1936–40), he wrote full-time. The books that resulted are the novels *Sugar in the air* and *Asleep in the afternoon*, and *The advance of the fungi*, his great history of plant diseases. It was then that he wrote the bulk of the essays and reviews that are listed in this bibliography and of which we reprint a selection in this book. The bibliography also lists the papers from his years of full-time employment as a plant scientist (1941–63). Although this listing is as complete as we can make it, there are surely omissions here.

Apart from a small poem, the first item in the bibliography is 'On watching an onion'. This was published in *The Week-end Review*, a new journal of liberal opinion that ran for four years (1930–4) before being taken over by *The New Statesman*, perhaps the archetypal British political-intellectual weekly of that period and on into the 1960s.

As Large remarks in his biographical note (p. 76), *The Week-end Review's* editor was Gerald Barry (1898–1968), a liberal journalist who went on to spend many years working at the *News Chronicle*, and who rose to greatest prominence – and a knighthood – as Director-General of the Festival of Britain in 1951.

'On watching an onion' suggests one aspect of the younger Large. It is a very consciously worked piece. Not only is the observer watching himself watch the onion, but we feel the writer is watching himself write the essay too. Large was at this time also writing a number of what I have called 'reveries' in the annotations in the bibliography, and which he called 'psychic adventures'. These are dreamy, surreal pieces, exploring further realms of consciousness. In the archive there are notes that show he was planning to publish these pieces himself, from his home, presumably in a very limited edition. His label for the collection reads 'HELL KITES | 13 psychic adventures | by E.C. Large | available from the author: 43 Avenue Gardens, Acton W3 | price 2/6 | pp. 72'.

The archive of Large's papers shows that he contemplated and worked on several other book projects. The novel 'Metame' exists in drafts dated around 1930. From a little earlier is a list of pieces, with word counts, that would form *A bonfire in the rain: collected sketches and impressions*. Later on, in the 1930s, he worked on pieces that report on his journeys as a rambler. This is the book, to be titled *Wind and wandering*, which might have followed *Asleep in the afternoon* into print, had that novel been more successful commercially.

Hell kites, the collection of the 'psychic adventures', seems never to have been issued, but in 1932 and 1933 some of these pieces were published in *The New English Weekly*. This was one of the two magazines that became E.C. Large's main vehicles of publication in the 1930s.

The New English Weekly was successor to *The New Age*, which since 1907 had been edited by A.R. Orage (at first with Holbrook Jackson). Orage (1873–1934) is an intriguing figure. He emerged in the turn-of-the-century socialist and literary culture of Leeds, from there coming to London to publish and edit *The New Age*, which soon became one of the central points of modern British culture in those years. Orage travelled through Ibsen, Nietzsche, Guild Socialism, and a sophisticated approach to literature, on to mysticism and especially the teachings of Gurdjieff, and also the Social Credit movement of C.H. Douglas. In 1932 he returned to editing with *The New English Weekly*. Large soon became a regular contributor, and the mixture of elements that Orage (and then his followers) brought to the journal must have been sympathetic: idiosyncratic socialist politics, a certain strain of metaphysics, close attention to linguistic expression.

The Adelphi, which became Large's other main means of publication, revolved around another strong and searching figure. John Middleton Murry (1889–1957) is best known for the parts he played in the lives of other writers, but he was also an extraordinarily prolific contributor on his own account. A 'man of letters' of a kind that could still exist at that time, his politics – pacifist, Tolstoyan, and engaging also with Marxism

The Week-end Review

of Politics, Books, The Theatre, Art and Music

Vol. I No. 1   MARCH 15, 1930   [Registered as a Newspaper]   6D

Contents

The Editorial and Business Offices of the WEEK-END REVIEW are at 229 Strand, London, W.C.2. The Subscription Rate is 30s. a year.

Comments of the Week

PINKING the Naval Conference with a caustic pen the other day, M. Henri de Jouvenal defined "Week-end" as "a period of the week in which the British Prime Minister is free to rest and the French Prime Minister is free to govern." For ordinary people the Week-end is a period in which they are free to read, and that is one reason why we have chosen the word as the title of this REVIEW. We will waste no space introducing ourselves. The work of months, planning a new paper, has in this instance been packed into days. The first number or two may show signs of the rush; if they do, we hope soon to remove them. In particular, we mean to add several features that take more time to arrange than we have yet had. But we do not seek indulgence. The choice of time was our own, and we stand for judgment as we are.

Return of the Prodigal

The political talk of the week is still of the Baldwin-Beaverbrook *rapprochement*. "The inevitability of gradualness" was never more picturesquely exemplified than in Mr. Baldwin's conduct in conceding Protection on the instalment system. "Line upon line, precept upon precept." Here a little, and there a little." Like all honest men, Mr. Baldwin has a touch of the fox about him. Or rather, as someone has nicely put it, he has plenty of peasant shrewdness.

Despite Lord Rothermere's vindictive tenacity, the collapse of the United Empire Party has delivered us from the bondage of newspaper government. It has also brought back into the limelight our old friend the Referendum. In a leading article we discuss the whole matter.

The Eternal Conference

On Sunday night the Prime Minister broadcast to the United States a very hopeful message on the Naval Conference. The general public, rigorously excluded from knowledge of the discussions, finds it difficult to share this confident optimism. The British and French Memoranda, issued last month, would hardly seem to justify it, seeing that the former proposes an increase of over 40,000 tons in the present British destroyer fleet, and one of 12,000 tons in its cruiser strength, while the figures claimed by France are so high that they can only have been put forward for bargaining purposes. We can understand the anxiety of delegates to convince their compatriots that a semi-failure is a startling success, but there is no reason why the Press should be a party to this conspiracy to hoodwink the public. To describe a Conference that results in increased cruiser tonnage for all the Powers concerned as a "Disarmament" Conference is to extenuate a euphemism. Despite these things, it is still too soon to call the Conference a failure. It cannot achieve the results predicted by the optimists, but the pessimists may even now be confounded. The usual

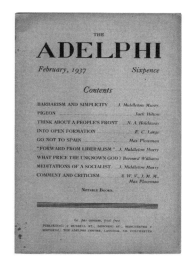

THE
ADELPHI

February, 1937   Sixpence

Contents

BARBARISM AND SIMPLICITY ...... *J. Middleton Murry*

PIGEON ...... *Jack Hilton*

THINK ABOUT A PEOPLE'S FRONT ...... *N. A. Holdaway*

INTO OPEN FORMATION ...... *E. C. Large*

GO NOT TO SPAIN ...... *Max Plowman*

"FORWARD FROM LIBERALISM" ...... *J. Middleton Murry*

WHAT PRICE THE UNKNOWN GOD ? *Bernard Williams*

MEDITATIONS OF A SOCIALIST ...... *J. Middleton Murry*

COMMENT AND CRITICISM ...... *A. W. V., J. M. M., Max Plowman*

NOTABLE BOOKS.

6*d.* per number, post free

PUBLISHING: 2 RUSSELL ST., DOWNING ST., MANCHESTER 2
EDITORIAL: THE ADELPHI CENTRE, LANGHAM, Nr. COLCHESTER

THE
NEW ENGLISH WEEKLY

A Review of Public Affairs, Literature and the Arts

Vol. V. No. 13   THURSDAY, JULY 12, 1934   SIXPENCE
Registered at G.P.O. as a Newspaper.

CONTENTS

SUMMER NOTICE

Publication of the "New English Weekly" will be suspended for the four weeks of August—9, 16, 23, 30 ; and will be resumed with the issue dated September 6.

Postal subscribers will be credited with the omitted four weeks' subscription.

Correspondence, both editorial and business, will be attended to as usual during the interval.

Notes of the Week

Until the Congressional elections are over, there is still time in which President Roosevelt may be brought to his senses. Already Senator Borah, one of the most influential politicians in the United States, has taken the field against the "Bureaucracy" involved in the President's present policy; and if only, in association with Senator Cutting and others in sympathy with Social Credit, Senator Borah can formulate a positive programme, there is still a chance that a genuinely democratic President may be persuaded to listen to it. Unfortu-

nately, Senator Borah is allowing himself for the moment to be manoeuvred into a position of direct opposition, which in times of emergency is almost always disadvantageous. It is well to criticise the policy of N.R.A. and to protest that it must lead to a form of centralised State control that first steals away the rights of the individual in the name of Dora and then taxes him to death in the name of Nora. But if the only alternative to the policy of Bureaucracy is a return to the status quo of unregulated individualism, then we may be sure that President Roosevelt's policy will triumph if only for the reason that it is new. To the criticism of President Roosevelt's policy it is necessary to add much more than a warning against its predictable results. Warnings alone seldom affect anybody. Side by side with the criticism it is necessary to set an alternative policy that is not only not a return to the status quo, but that is equally calculated to avoid the evils of Bureaucracy and positively to lead to a more complete realisation of economic democracy— the policy of Social Credit, in short. This should and Christianity – came to the fore in the 1930s. *The Adelphi* in its 'new series' (published from 1930) was more than a journal. In his auto-biographical note, Large refers to the Murry's 'precious "Universitas"'. This was The Adelphi Centre at Langham in Essex. Readers and contributors were invited there for regular weekend conferences and for summer schools. The train and bus times for Londoners travelling to the Centre were given on the back of the magazine. Among those who were billed as giving lectures at Adelphi summer schools were John Macmurray, Herbert Read, F. R. Leavis, T. S. Eliot, Karl Polanyi. At the summer school of 1937, Large spoke on 'Mercury, sulphur, salt'. Reading *The Adelphi*, one has the sense of The Adelphi Centre as a place of genuine education and self-help. And though the scenes in *Asleep in the afternoon* that are obviously based on the Centre have a satirical flavour, it is clear that Large was very fond of the place and what it was trying for.

Large makes an appearance in Rayner Heppenstall's memoir *Four absentees*, in a description of the 1937 summer school: 'The colloidal chemist was on his feet, a big, brown-faced man with a French-type moustache and bobbed black hair (he tells me this is now white).'[2] Heppenstall also says that it was Murry who helped to place *Sugar in the air* with its publisher, Jonathan Cape ('the publisher cabled his offer from somewhere in mid-Atlantic'). Another writer in the Adelphi circle was George Orwell, who must have met Large first at Langham. Readers of Orwell's letters will come across this intriguing remark: 'I was greatly impressed by Large, whom no doubt you know, and my wife almost fell in love with him when he came to tea here.'[3]

In the biographical note, E. C. Large provided his own concise account of his career as a writer. The bibliography given here fleshes out the picture with details of the published work. I have also added, at the end of the bibliography, a list of writings that discuss his books. One sees that his two novels of the 1930s are treated as 'scientific romances', the term that was devised for the specifically British fiction of the period 1890–1950 (the span covered in Brian Stableford's book on the subject), whose defining figure was H. G. Wells. The third novel, *Dawn in Andromeda*, is more clearly 'science fiction'. So Large as a novelist has been included in encyclopedias of science fiction, not touching the literary mainstream. But it is Large's position outside the mainstream that seems so attractive and valuable now.

Robin Kinross

Notes

1. Norman Potter, *What is a designer* (fourth edition, London: Hyphen Press, 2002, pp. 39, 169).

2. Rayner Heppenstall, *Four absentees* (London: Barrie & Rockliff, 1960, p. 134). The twenty pages of this chapter give a vivid description of the author's experiences at the Centre.

3. Letter to Jack Common, 5 October 1936. *George Orwell, The collected essays, journalism and letters* (Harmondsworth: Penguin Books, 1970, vol. 1, p. 263).

Bibliography

* *Indicates inclusion in this volume, reset according to the published versions; unpublished texts are shown in reproductions of archived typescripts.*

1929

'Spendthrift', *The Bermondsey Book*, vol. 6, no. 4, September–November 1929, p. 9 [poem]

1930

* 'On watching an onion', *The Week-end Review*, 20 September 1930, pp. 372–3 [essay in the phenomenology of perception]

1932

'Hippodrome', *New English Weekly*, vol. 1, no. 12, 7 July 1932, p. 281 [reverie]

. . . .

'May noon', *New English Weekly*, vol. 1, no. 24, 29 September 1932, pp. 569–70 [story of rambling]

1933

* 'Escape, 1918', *The Adelphi* (new series), vol. 7, no. 2, November 1933, pp. 96–100 [autobiographical]

. . . .

'Gillymot', *New English Weekly*, vol. 2, no. 14, 19 January 1933, p. 327 [reverie]

. . . .

'Royal Roger', *New English Weekly*, vol. 3, no. 15, 27 July 1933, p. 348 [reverie]

. . . .

* 'The adequate tigers', *New English Weekly*, vol. 3, no. 17, 10 August 1933, p. 396 [reverie]

. . . .

* 'Our modern Hesiod', *New English Weekly*, vol. 3, no. 26, 12 October 1933, pp. 608–10 [on Irish state agricultural publications]

. . . .

'Derry air', *New English Weekly*, vol. 4, no. 4, 9 November 1933, p. 95 [poem]

. . . .

'A word tax', *The Week-end Review*, 3 June 1933, pp. 627–8 [proposal]

1934

* 'Journey through Denmark', *The Adelphi* (new series), vol. 8, no. 6, September 1934, pp. 400–407 [travel report]

. . . .

'Song', *New English Weekly*, vol. 4, no. 16, 1 February 1934, p. 377 [poem]

'The power of England', *New English Weekly*, vol. 5, no. 13, 12 July 1934, pp. 294–6 [how money works in England]

. . . .

'Trespassing', *New English Weekly*, vol. 5, no. 15, 26 July 1934, p. 348 [poem]

. . . .

'Malt, more malt', *New English Weekly*, vol. 5, no. 23, 20 September 1934, pp. 446–7 [a plan to market malt]

. . . .

'The distribution of leisure' (part 1), *New English Weekly*, vol. 6, no. 11, 27 December 1934, pp. 230–1 [another view of unemployment]

. . . .

'Root carver', *The Countryman*, October 1934, p. 287 [fragment]

1935

'Death's little finger', *The Adelphi* (new series), vol. 10, no. 6, September 1935, pp. 336–41 [autobiographical]

. . . .

'The distribution of leisure' (part 2), *New English Weekly*, vol. 6, no. 12, 3 January 1935, pp. 257–8

. . . .

'The distribution of leisure', *New English Weekly*, vol. 6, no. 15, 24 January 1935, pp. 324 [letter, in reply to criticism from R. L. Northridge in issue of 17 January]

. . . .

'Registered Marks' (part 1), *New English Weekly*, vol. 6, no. 25, 4 April 1935, pp. 512–13 [report on a visit to Germany]

. . . .

'Registered Marks' (part 2), *New English Weekly*, vol. 6, no. 26, 11 April 1935, pp. 530–1

. . . .

'Why pay income tax?', *New English Weekly*, vol. 7, no. 5, 16 May 1935, p. 86 [ways of optimizing income tax payments]

. . . .

'Given a corpse ... or the Sayer's saga', *New English Weekly*, vol. 7, no. 16, 1 August 1935, pp. 308–10 [on Dorothy Sayers]

. . . .

* 'St. Thomas De Quincey', *New English Weekly*, vol. 8, no. 10, 19 December 1935, pp. 189–90 [review of Malcolm Elwin, *De Quincey*]

1936

'Dog days in Catalonia', *The Adelphi* (new series), vol. 12, no. 6, September 1936, pp. 337–42 [travel report]

. . . .

* 'Hypnagogic hallucinations', *The Aryan Path*, vol. 7, no. 7, July 1936, pp. 305–8 [essay]

. . . .

'Kindred', *New English Weekly*, vol. 8, no. 16, 30 January 1936, p. 306 [poem]

. . . .

'Some pleasures of the pit', *New English Weekly*, vol. 8, no. 16, 30 January 1936, pp. 309–10 [review of Group Theatre productions]

. . . .

'Hell's Passover', *New English Weekly*, vol. 9, no. 3, 30 April 1936, pp. 46–7 [on air-raid precaution literature]

. . . .

'About the working class', *New English Weekly*, vol. 10, no. 10, 17 December 1936, pp. 188–9 [review of John Strachey, *Theory and practice of Communism*]

. . . .

'Sever the earth', *New English Weekly*, vol. 10, no. 11, 24 December 1936, p. 217 [review of Jacques Spitz, *Sever the earth*]

1937

Sugar in the air, London: Jonathan Cape [novel] (New York: Charles Scribner's, 1937) (London: Hyphen Press, 2008)

    Reviews: *The Adelphi* (new series), vol. 13, no. 9, June 1937, p. 384 [J.M.M.] — *The London Mercury*, vol. 36, no. 213, July 1937, pp. 298–9 [V.M.L. Scott] — *New English Weekly*, vol. 14, no. 10, 15 December 1938, pp. 153–4 [Upton Sinclair] — *The New Republic*, 8 September 1937, pp. 139–40 [Otis Ferguson] — *The Spectator*, 11 June 1937, p. 1116 — *Times Literary Supplement*, 26 June 1937, pp. 479–80

. . . .

* 'Hail!', *The Adelphi* (new series), vol. 13, no. 4, January 1937, pp. 196–8

. . . .

* 'Into open formation', *The Adelphi* (new series), vol. 13, no. 5, February 1937, pp. 236–8 [on different kinds of pacifism]

. . . .

'Peace', *The Adelphi* (new series), vol. 13, no. 6, March 1937, pp. 277–8 [autobiographical fragments describing contentment]

* 'OHMS', *The Adelphi* (new series), vol. 13, no. 7, April 1937, pp. 308–10 [caustic reflections on a British Army recruiting film]

. . . .

'Adults only', *The Adelphi* (new series), vol. 13, no. 10, July 1937, pp. 410–11 [reverie]

. . . .

'Towards Tolstoy', *The Adelphi* (new series), vol. 13, no. 11, August 1937, pp. 428–31 [meditations, recommending Tolstoy's views]

. . . .

* 'The Stour Valley', *The Adelphi* (new series), vol. 14, no. 2, November 1937, pp. 50–8 [travel report]

. . . .

book review, *The Adelphi* (new series), vol. 14, no. 3, December 1937, pp. 93–4 [David Jones, *In parenthesis*]

. . . .

book review, *The Adelphi* (new series), vol. 14, no. 3, December 1937, pp. 94–5 [James Harvey Robinson, *The human comedy*]

. . . .

book review, *The Adelphi* (new series), vol. 14, no. 3, December 1937, pp. 96 [*The mind in chains*]

. . . .

* 'In defence of Mr Baldwin', *New English Weekly*, vol. 10, no. 13, 7 January 1937, p. 260 [letter about the Abdication]

. . . .

'The world of science', *New English Weekly*, vol. 10, no. 17, 4 February 1937, pp. 331–2 [review of F. Sherwood Taylor, *The world of science*]

. . . .

'Economist and layman', *New English Weekly*, vol. 10, no. 19, 18 February 1937, pp. 371–2 [review of W. H. Hutt, *Economists and the public*]

. . . .

'Aerial defence', *New English Weekly*, vol. 10, no. 19, 18 February 1937, pp. 374–5 [on air-raid precautions]

. . . .

'Newts', *New English Weekly*, vol. 10, no. 23, 18 March 1937, p. 448 [review of Karel Capek, *War with the newts*]

. . . .

'Close-up of Mammon', *New English Weekly*, vol. 10, no. 24, 25 March 1937, p. 466 [review of F. D. Klingender & Stuart Legg, *Money behind the screen*]

. . . .

'The Hanks predictor', *New English Weekly*, vol. 10, no. 26, 8 April 1937, p. 509–10 [on a device to assist anti-aircraft shooting]

'The sceptical physicist', *New English Weekly*, vol. 11, no. 5, 13 May 1937, pp. 92–3 [review of Albert Eagle, *The philosophy of religion versus the philosophy of science*]

. . . .

'Radioactivity', *New English Weekly*, vol. 11, no. 11, 24 June 1937, pp. 209–10 [review of Rudolf Brunngraber, *Radium*]

. . . .

'The problem of the mesh', *New English Weekly*, vol. 11, no. 14, 15 July 1937, pp. 269–70 [review of E. Ford, *The nation's sea-fish supply*]

. . . .

'Science and the absolute', *New English Weekly*, vol. 11, no. 26, 7 October 1937, pp. 431–2 [review of James Harvey Robinson, *The human comedy*; Robert Boyle, *The sceptical chymist*; A. Cornelius, *The logical structure of science*; W. H. George, *The scientist in action*]

. . . .

* 'Ten thousand faces', *New English Weekly*, vol. 12, no. 1, 14 October 1937, pp. 9–10 [reflections on keeping a stand for a chemical company at a flower show]

. . . .

* 'Children on the Mappin Terrace', *New English Weekly*, vol. 12, no. 7, 25 November 1937, pp. 131–2 [review of C. W. Kimmins, *Children's dreams*; Marjorie Thorburn, *Child at play*]

. . . .

* 'The Coronation Mass-Observed', *New English Weekly*, vol. 12, no. 12, 30 December 1937, pp. 231–2 [review of *May 12: Mass-Observation day survey*]

1938
Asleep in the afternoon, London: Jonathan Cape [novel]
(New York: Henry Holt, 1939)
(London: Hyphen Press, 2008)
      Reviews: *The Adelphi* (new series), vol. 15, no. 1, October 1938, pp. 46–7 [Geoffrey West] — *New English Weekly*, vol. 14, no. 10, 15 December 1938, pp. 153–4 [Upton Sinclair] — *Times Literary Supplement*, 20 August 1938, p. 541

. . . .

* 'The ten commandments', *The Adelphi* (new series), vol. 14, no. 9, June 1938, pp. 282–5

. . . .

* 'The semantic discipline', *New English Weekly*, vol. 13, no. 6, 19 May 1938, pp. 111–12 [review of Stuart Chase, *The tyranny of words*]

'Pierre and Marie Curie', *New English Weekly*, vol. 13, no. 10, 16 June 1938, pp. 191–2 [review of Eve Curie, *Madame Curie: a biography*]

. . . .

'Song of Pittsburgh', *New English Weekly*, vol. 13, no. 25, 29 September 1938, p. 374 [review of Haniel Long, *Pittsburgh memoranda*]

. . . .

'Summons – and substance', *New English Weekly*, vol. 13, no. 26, 6 October 1938, pp. 389–90 [review of John Middleton Murry, *Heaven – and earth*]

1939
'Night shift', *New English Weekly*, vol. 14, no. 16, 26 January 1939, pp. 238–40 [story of workers in an iron/steel foundry]

. . . .

'Come to an end', *New English Weekly*, vol. 16, no. 2, pp. 24–5, 26 October 1939, pp. 24–5 [review of Frances Bellerby, *Come to an end, and other stories*]

1940
The advance of the fungi, London: Jonathan Cape [history]
(New York: Henry Holt, 1940)
(New York: Dover Books, 1962)
(St Paul, MN: American Phytopathological Society, 2003)
      Reviews: *The Adelphi* (new series), vol. 17, no. 11, August 1941, p. 399 [R. Murry] — *Economic History Review*, vol. 11, no. 1, 1941, pp. 112–13 [G. E. Fussell] — *Inoculum*, vol. 55, no. 4, September 2004 [Britt Bunyard] (and at: www.namyco.org/book_reviews/Advance_of_the_Fungi.html) — *Isis*, vol. 34, no. 3, 1943, pp. 23–2 [Morris C. Leikind] — *Quarterly Review of Biology*, vol. 16, no. 3, 1941, p. 364 [anon.] — *The Scientific Monthly*, vol. 53, no. 4, 1941, pp. 378–9 [John W. Roberts] — *Times Literary Supplement*, 8 March 1941, p. 118

. . . .

'Success story', *New English Weekly*, vol. 17, no. 25, 10 October 1940, pp. 279–80 [review of A. S. Eve, *Rutherford: being the life and letters of the Right Hon. Lord Rutherford, O. M.*]

. . . .

'A fiftieth of an acre', *New English Weekly*, vol. 18, no. 1, 24 October 1940, pp. 5–6 [autobiographical]

14

1941

'Potato blight', *Journal of the Ministry of Agriculture and Fisheries*, vol. 48, pp. 22–8

1943

'Control of potato blight (*Phyophthora infestans*) by spraying with suspensions of metallic copper', *Nature*, vol. 151, pp. 80–1

1945

'Field trials of copper fungicides for the control of potato blight. 1. Foliage protection and yield', *Annals of Applied Biology*, vol. 32, pp. 319–29

1952

'Trials of substitutes for sulphuric acid for potato haulm killing', *Plant Pathology*, vol. 1, pp. 2–9

. . . .

'Surveys for choke (*Epichloe typhina*) in cockfoot seed crops, 1951', *Plant Pathology*, vol. 1, pp. 23–8 [compiled by ECL]

. . . .

'The interpretation of progress curves for potato blight and other plant diseases', *Plant Pathology*, vol. 1, pp. 109–17

1953

'Potato blight forecasting investigation in England and Wales, 1950–1952', *Plant Pathology*, vol. 2, pp. 1–15

. . . .

'The distribution of spray deposits in low-volume potato spraying', *Plant Pathology*, vol. 2, pp. 93–8 [ECL with G.G. Taylor]

1954

'Surveys for choke (*Epichloe typhina*) in Cocksfoot seed crops, 1951–53', *Plant Pathology*, vol. 3, pp. 6–11 [compiled by ECL]

. . . .

'Spraying trials in the potato-growing area around The Wash, 1948–53', *Plant Pathology*, vol. 3, pp. 40–8 [ECL with R. Eric Taylor, I.E. Storey and A.H. Yule]

. . . .

'Trials of substitutes for sulphuric acid for potato haulm killing, 1952 and 1953, *Plant Pathology*, vol. 3, pp. 90–9 [compiled by ECL]

. . . .

'Growth stages in cereals: illustration of the Feekes scale', *Plant Pathology*, vol. 3, pp. 128–9

1955

'Methods of plant-disease measurement and forecasting in Great Britain', *Annals of Applied Biology*, vol. 42, pp. 344–54

. . . .

'Survey of common scab of potatoes in Great Britain, 1952 and 1953', *Plant Pathology*, vol. 4, pp. 1–8 [ECL with June K. Honey]

1956

Dawn in Andromeda, London: Jonathan Cape [novel]
   Reviews: *Times Literary Supplement*, 27 July 1956, p. 445 — *Transactions of the British Mycological Society*, vol. 39, p. 507 [P.H. Gregory]

. . . .

'Potato blight forecasting and survey work in England and Wales, 1953–55', *Plant Pathology*, vol. 5, pp. 39–52 [compiled by ECL]

1958

'Losses caused by potato blight in England and Wales', *Plant Pathology*, vol. 7, pp. 39–48 [compiled by ECL]

. . . .

'Surveys of clover rot with incidental observations on eelworm in clover: England and Wales, 1953–55', *Plant Pathology*, vol. 7, pp. 115–24 [compiled by ECL and others]

1960

Potato blight epidemics throughout the world, Washington DC: Agricultural Research Bureau [ECL with A.E. Cox]

1961

'Disease losses in potatoes', *Proceedings of the Nutrition Society*, vol. 20, pp. 15–20

. . . .

'Pursuits of mycology', *Transactions of the British Mycological Society*, vol. 44, pp. 1–23

. . . .

'Extent of protective spraying and haulm destruction on potato crops in Great Britain, 1952–60', *Plant Pathology*, vol. 10, pp. 96–100 [ECL with Rachel A. Waines]

1962

'The measurement of cereal mildew and its effect on yield', *Plant Pathology*, vol. 11, pp. 47–57 [ECL with D.A. Doling]

1966

'Measuring plant diseases', *Annual Review of Phytopathology*, vol. 4, pp. 9–26

1967

W.P.K. Findlay, *Wayside and woodland fungi*, London: Frederick Warne [includes 20 colour illustrations by ECL)

COMMENTARY

1968

W.H.G. Armytage, *Yesterday's tomorrows: a historical survey of future societies*, London: Routledge & Kegan Paul, 1968 [on ECL, pp. 165–7]

1977

P.H. Gregory & F.J.H. Moore, 'Ernest Charles Large', *Transactions of the British Mycological Society*, vol. 69, pp. 167–70

1982

'Plant pathology: E.C. Large and phytopathometry', *Plant Pathology*, vol. 31, pp. 7–8

1985

Brian Stableford, *Scientific romance in Britain 1890–1950*, London: Fourth Estate [on ECL, pp. 259–60]

1989

Walter Gratzer (ed.), *The literary companion to science*, Harlow: Longman, 1989

1991

Noelle Watson & Paul E. Schellinger (ed.), *Twentieth-century science fiction writers*, Chicago: St James Press [Karen Charmaine Blansfield on ECL, p. 469]

1993

John Clute & Peter Nicholls (ed.), *The encyclopedia of science fiction*, London: Orbit [Brian Stableford on ECL, p. 691]

. . . .

J. Colhoun, 'Ernest Charles Large: pioneer in phytopathometry', *Annual Review of Phytopathology*, vol. 31, pp. 23–31

On watching an onion

At first I saw the onion as a globe fish standing on its nose, a Chianti bottle with a broken neck, or the lower part of an obese old woman; but with a steady seriousness I set these evasions of thought aside and regarded the onion for its own sake, the example of its own virtue. It was soon clear to me that it might become a monster. It challenged me, and with my whole mentality I could no more remove it or delete it from consciousness than it could remove or delete me. It set up a conflict between my senses and I, and in the fixity of my regard I conceived that my eyes would go out to it and meet it in mid-field with a violent explosion and inconceivable consequences.

No one can doubt that there is a secret locked in an onion; that our contemplation is pitiful in its inevitable failure to perceive it; that we deride all watchers of onions in self-defence, as gazers after the unknowable that it discomforts us to acknowledge. But why believe more of an onion than can be perceived? Why is it flippant to speak of its chemical composition or its depictable form? May not the imperceivable itself arise only from an inherent human belief in the fecundity of the unknown? But that is one more evasion to discourage a dislike research. Certainly the onion has a secret, a reason for its existence, but we believe it can never be surprised. We make that confession with pride and call it wisdom, but it only justifies evasion.

The whole joyous equipage of philosophy is brought to a dead stop by an onion. It has only to lie in the way and dumbly interrogate: what of me? And all our concepts and hypotheses, physics and metaphysics, may return to the circus together. For the proper prevention of this insult to humanity every moral, religious and neighbourly taboo conspires to anathematize the watching of onions. It is heretical, obscene and finally daft. Heretical to believe that anything can be seen of an unknown region apportioned to God; obscene to bring Freud and an onion together; and daft to sit for hours before a disinterred pot-herb.

The most abstruse and fundamental quality I could perceive in the onion was its weight, its utter immobility on an upturned dish; but the onion at least discovered *fear* in me. The onion and I were in an empty house, and when the onion was magnified and trembling in my steady regard, my eye muscles strained and something clearly about to happen, I was afraid and looked aside. Of what use was my contemplation if I dare not resign and entrust myself to all that might ensue: hypnosis or hysteria? I scryed as the virtuous play at adventure, guarding my safe return. And above that root fear of new experience rode a host of petty fears; the apprehension of faces at the windows, and a lively misgiving born of popguns and jokes at school.

I applied the cautious methods of experimental science. Once every hour I observed the onion for four minutes and then recorded my impressions. Is not that the authentic method – catalogues and inference? But when I came to draw the inferences, I found that they concerned myself and not the onion. What had an onion to do with my familiar, all-too-human indecencies, or with the scenes of past experience that it revived for me? Whose were the meadow saffrons on the Mendip Hills? Mine. As much mine as the particular glint and surface of the seventh onion skin is intimately the onion's. Of the onion, science vouchsafed nothing but the presence of a body modifying the light from the lamp. I had done as much with one unsophisticated eye. True I remembered that the onion is a monocotyledon of the family Allium, but I am also a vertebrate, and my second name is Charles – does that discover me?

Science stands proud of the onion, preoccupied with itself. But what of the primeval savage who first encountered the onion, said 'yung-yung' or some such thing in answer to its pungency, and expressed for all time the feeling of the *genus homo* for the *genus allium*. So, say the vitalists, there is nothing more that can be known – they say that with great intensity, and evade the onion with exceeding glory to themselves.

Clearly it would be useless to approach or dissect the onion, that would be naïve. I went to bed. There I had a far more subtle method. An appearance to which I had so persistently exposed my visual nerve ends during the day might be hoped to reanimate them at night and drift out before me in the field of residual images in some revealing and distinctive character. I closed my eyes, and immediately a dense tangle of pine needles swept across the field, followed by different kinds of electromagnets, and crocus sprouts on flower beds. Even my own nerves and visual sensory organism conspired against the onion. Perhaps in some dim aeon of the imagined past, when the anthropoid embryo was a marine worm, the very nerves had learned the wisdom of ignoring 'what must not be known'. Only after a long time, and then only in a remote corner of the phantasmagoria, did I see any likeness of an onion.

I passed into dreams while watching for more. I was inside an onion, a spacious, lofty onion, like the reading room of the British Museum, but within the onion only the tedium and headache of contemplation were dramatized. In the morning I recalled the other onion that had appeared in the visions of my semi-slumbers. It had shoots, it was green. Ah-ha! cried the already-bored feminine in me, *there*'s the secret of the onion – its potentiality of growth, its tender, upspringing shoots. So I need not bother any more. But sentimentality is as bad a loosener of the conscience as similes and science. I returned to the contemplation of the onion, not without a further discouragement from the eternally feminine – it is useless, she said, to stare at the onion, you must wait and take by surprise. Wait, in fact, until the onion came to me – another excuse to evade it as it lay before me.

It was as barren and unsatisfying as a painted Madonna in a shrine, I might prostrate myself or bring tears into my eyes, but there would be no more than the familiar place and the must of furniture. Ingenious the thought that I and the onion were one; the onion a

mere content of my consciousness. But the consciousness would be a frame with no glass in it between me and the onion, an entirely independent invention that might be lifted out and played with at some other time. For me there was the onion on its upturned dish, altering somewhat in definition with the fatigue of my eyes, but not otherwise subjective to me; there was the onion I could think of, but not see, with my eyes shut; and lastly, there was the onion of my *hallucinations hypnagogiques*. No doubt, I might also, by a happy twist of words, evoke the onion as a poetic image. A mystagogue might fit a frame round any of these, and say the onion has been *apprehended* in *sensation; represented* by the *imagination*; or *conceived* as *reality* in *consciousness*. ... But it would be a stupid pretentious frame, one more device to divert me from the insufficiency of the picture. There would be no soul-of-an-onion in it, and nothing to philosophize about if we were steadily aware of that.

There is only one way to treat a thing that pricks one's divine afflatus, and that is to destroy it. It gives us pain, psychologically speaking, and we destroy it in self-defence. I cut the onion up, very deliberately, and cooked it in boiling oil. Then I ate it, not because of any savage belief that its virtues would enter my *consciousness* via the oesophagus but because in no other way could I so completely destroy it as an object of contemplation.

The Week-end Review, 20 September 1930, pp. 372–3

<u>Notes on the story of Metame</u>.   29.5.30

<u>Format</u>   Could well be about the size of Carl and Anna, by Leonard Frank.
200 words per page, 110 pages. 22,000 words.   As the subject requires greater
breadth of treatment perhaps 35,000 words. 140 typewritten pages.

<u>Theme</u>   The transition from the heart-whole surrender to of first love to the
compromise of marriage.

<u>Characterisation</u>   The first person I, used very sparingly. The dissociated
Metame.   The first beloved--Agnes.   The wife--Minorca.   The unborn babe--
Benjamin.   The "I" is emotionless and eternal.   Metame is vaccilatory in his
passions, and kaliedescopic in his surroundings.   Everything to him is sensuous
full of colour, movement and sound.   Agnes is realistic, her incongruity is
accepted.   Minorca is realistic, she accepts but is not accepted.   The phantasy
of a perfect comrade or lover, after Agnes, is not personified.   Benjamin is
thought created.

<u>The Issue</u>   Marriage.   The book begins and ends with marriage.   The interest
centres on the issue, to be or not to be.   And marriage is finally destroyed, not
the first personal "I".

<u>Background</u>   The Gower coast.   The welsh people supplying the fantastic diversit
of Metame experience.   The book starts in London and returns to London again.
references to excursions out of Wales, etc. are carefully subdued.

The Metame experiences as written are excellently well coloured. It remains to
write the first personal I " parts from the view point of an older and more
sophisticated"I". The book is thus synthetic.

Outline for the novel 'Metame' (256 × 205 mm), which was unpublished and probably
unfinished. Handwritten drafts of the text exist in the archive, some dated 1930.
Chapter 1 opens: 'The boat for Lucerne came bearing in to the quay...'

Escape, 1918

It is my good fortune that I never went to France, nor was I wounded or apparently hurt in any way by the War. No one dear to me was mutilated, nor did the shadow of death lay waste my adolescence. I was sixteen and had not long left school when the last shot was fired; I have the War to thank for setting the course of my life, and giving me my first taste of self-determination. Throughout the War, which I thought would never end, I felt the age for calling up coming closer and closer, and I anticipated it with a stupid unquestioning resistance. Patriotism or no patriotism, I determined that for myself I would never participate in the murders of Flanders. There was no nobility of any kind in my attitude, nor could I have sustained it, in the face of every opposition, at that age, if I had not been accustomed to exert a dogged and solitary resistance. I felt myself weaker and poorer than my schoolfellows and forced to defend myself. It was not in my nature to fight it out with them, I went by back streets to avoid their bullying and snatched my education in spite of them.

So, when I saw conscription inevitably approaching, it was only another form of brutality, and it was natural for me to meet it in the same way. As a last resort I determined to smash my kneecaps with a dumb-bell, for I had read that that would incapacitate me for a long time; but it was grim and required courage. I searched for alternatives as desperately as a cornered rat seeks for a hole, and I found out the munition factories. There was just a chance that I might make myself 'indispensable', as they called it, and so avoid both the dumb-bell and the guns.

But for the War I should have entered my father's profession and become a lawyer, but a trend of ingenuity and a boyish delight in mechanics assisted me, and I worked night and day for 'indispensability' in engineering. It became my goal and I pursued it secretly;

at school they were not likely to help me, in fact they told me in so many words: St Paul's is not a trade school.

The war delirium raged in the school, and the boys at fourteen were forced, coerced and intimidated into the OTC. The boy officers fed to France were the glory of the School, and there was not one who dared raise a dissentient voice. It was *done* to go, that was all about it; to refuse would be to let down the School. One of the masters, late of the regular army, and too old himself ever to face the guns, assumed high command and bullied the few protesting boys into the corps. I was amongst them. The corps was not the Army and I lied to them. My zeal to become an officer in the Royal Engineers was quite extraordinary. They pushed me ahead with mathematics, let me into the workshops, and all the resources of the school were available to me. In the evenings I wandered about the side streets of Fulham and Hammersmith looking for munition works.

For months I turned up on the corps parades, and marched up and down obediently with a dummy rifle. It was better than having to play Rugby, for I could get through the stupid motions of the drill easily enough, and the others had less chance of making me their butt. The puttees gaped a little on my spindle legs, but that joke was soon stale. It is strange how conscious I was of legs at that time, my own, and those of my schoolfellows. I know now that it was fear of the shock of the dumb-bell and fear of the awful thing that I should have to do, that really obsessed me, but at that time I thought it the terror and pathos of War. The wounded came back and I saw them in the streets with a flap of empty trouser pinned up to a thigh. There was space where the leg should have been, and I looked through at the traffic and the pavement with trembling supernatural horror. Perhaps, had I been to France, I should quickly have grown callous to amputations, but I was not callous.

From my earliest years I had liked to roam about the fields and commons. Nobody embarrassed or mocked at me there, and often I believe I walked in a kind of dream. When I wrote essays about the grass and the yellow flowers tears would come into my eyes. Our home was a very disturbed one, and my days on the common with a packet of sandwiches were about the sweetest experience I had known. The War would destroy that – it aimed at the legs. There were recruiting posters on the walls then, where Lord Derby made the jokes of a bully in power: 'Will you march too or wait till March 2', he said. I thought of the yellow flowers, the dumb-bell, and the empty trouser legs, and my sullen resistance quickened into hate. After that they could have flayed me alive before I would go to France.

The months went on and I worked against the school, rankling with my enormous sour secret, to become exempt and 'indispensable.' My devices sometimes were bitterly amusing – I would play truant from prayers, to be kept in and do machine drawing in the art-school; and when it came to firing the compulsory shots, provided by the War Office, I let them all off at 'two o'clock' on the outside ring of the target, to avoid marks for proficiency. But I turned up on the parades and won prizes for engineering, so that the valorous Captain of our OTC was pleased with me on the whole, and sure I should get my commission.

During the summer of 1918 I went to a great number of factories, asking for munition work. I had no idea of what was being done, or what job I might hope to get; the streets were squalid and smelly, the people very vulgar, I felt I was going down into the muck, into some foul and vicious pit of degradation. I would stand by the works' clock, with my school cap in my hand, waiting in a blushing perspiration of fright for the Works Manager. The girls in the time office would lean over their desks and giggle between themselves: 'College cuckoo! College bum!'

By curious good luck, I was refused in turn by all the mushroom works that were turning out shells, and an old-established firm of engineers, of good repute, took me apprentice to fitting and turning. They are skilled trades, and with a little attention to the lowering of my general health, I should certainly have been exempt, C3 perhaps, and 'Indispensable'.

Accustomed to the evasions of a suburban home, and the cultural upholstery of a public school, my first few weeks in the shops were an experience of unparalleled fatigue and horror. The working hours seemed nearly endless, and the tasks monotony mad. We turned pulleys by the hundred, spindles by the thousand, and screws and pins by the hundreds of thousands. The piles grew and dwindled in the racks like great pyramids, and often in an agony of impatience we found ourselves watching and rearranging the piles with an insane attention, to make them bigger, or less or more symmetrical. The cutting oil, burnt by the hot spirals of turnings, smelled heavy and rancid, and the noise about us was as loud as the endless passing of a train. But worst of all was the apparent viciousness of my workmates: their words were steeped in filth; their slang drawn from excrement, everything with double meanings. The women were lewder than the men, and went much more directly to the point. They only brought me face to face with my own nature, but it was many years before I came to thank them for that.

There was a girl called 'Ginger' who used to drive the crane. They would crowd under her as she climbed down the ladder, and whistle and call after her as she went to the lavatory. One day, in the dinner hour, they took off her things, and laid her stark naked on some sacks on a tool box. One or two of us were 'pi', and seeing us shamefaced, she leered and made as if to offer herself to us, but we broke away and there was a great guffaw. But they were not all like Ginger, and very soon I had learned to stiffen the effeminate public school accent and be both blasphemous and timidly obscene. I split words to put oaths in the middle – Hammer-bloody-smith – but for my knowledge of life I might have been a child. The girls on the automatics, of my own age and less, seemed responsible women already, and sometimes would befriend me in a practical way. One morning there was a great struggling at the canteen window for potato cakes. I jostled indeterminately on the fringe of the crowd, when a girl got up from her food, took my twopence, and presently shoved the cakes into my hand.

In a week or two I had appreciated that no one bothered much about me, the persecutions of school life were not continued, the team spirit was absent. Nobody cared a hang for athletics, social conformity or dubious glory; it was each for himself for the piecework money. I was left alone, except by the foreman and a tough old tradesman who was paid a little to give an eye to my machine as well as his own. It was not difficult to work for indispensability when everybody else was working for money. The fear of the dumb-bell died away without seeming to fix itself under my consciousness, for I knew that I should be safe enough. It did not occur to me that it was more merciful to fire in France than to work at the lathes. I thought only of myself. And from my security I even ventured to raise my ladder over the massacre into the bedizened future. I determined to go on among open-mouthed men and raw materials, in the surf of new knowledge, to become a chemist or an engineer. I suffered the purification of War.

Three months after I had started in the works the Armistice was declared. The news came down the shops like a paralysing wind. It was a joke, it could not be true. Then came confirmation and certainty. We knocked out the switches; the motors whined down; doors were flung open and we ran into the road. From all over London came the sound of shouting. The munition girls ran about with rattles and children's toys bought from the depleted shops. I stood outside the works, watching the people running, and suddenly I began to run with them, saying over and over to myself with a voice that was not my own: 'We have won the War; oh lovely God, we have won the War ... .'

The Adelphi (new series), vol.7, no.2, November 1933, pp. 96–100

The adequate tigers

The tigers passed and repassed in their chamber. As I walked up and down, in the dry heat, I could see them, yellow and lethargic, sliding against each other, with hang-dog heads and velvet tails. Day after day I paced before the cage, counting my steps, and returning when I reached the walls. The iron bars were black and square, and met in perspective above me. The stairs were open to the public but I could not escape. My eyes were fixed on the tigers, my feet harnessed to the floor.

They never slept nor angered; never seemed aware of me; but slunk endlessly round, in the privacy of their shadows, sullen and unappeased. I pressed my face between the bars; thrust them my arm up to the shoulder, but the white flesh would not excite them. They were heavy and hungerless.

'You must go in to them,' the keeper said, 'go in to them'.

He was presumptuous, and I shrank from his advances; once he dragged me by the arm:

'Look!' he cried, 'the man-eaters.'

'It is a zebra,' I said.

'But the velvet paws', he cried, 'the velvet paws!'

'It is a leopard,' I said.

But I knew they were tigers and I clung to the bars, trembling in my ecstasy.

*

The tigers wheeled at the God-head, violent above their chasms, running, black and yellow, in a lustre of fur. Their hunger swelled and sank, as thunder sweeps the clouds.

I ran upon the steps, and, there, leaping from bar to bar of the quicksilvered cage, I saw the imprisoned image of my face: the lips withdrawn from my clenched teeth and the eyebrows high above my focussed eyes.

*

I paced again, and the bars were black iron. Between the tigers and I there intervened a medium of isinglass. It was transparent but impassable; a vibrant cliff of jelly. I beat it with my hands, pulled at the suspended masses, but I knew they would dissolve only in thought. As I clambered about the substance, peering in the quaking cracks and facets, I could see the tigers, sometimes magical in prisms, sometimes dull as daylight.

I was impatient and tried every trick: displayed erudition, supposed and pretended; wept, prayed and angered, but the substance was impassable. No matter what entrainment I chose, what manner of association, only the stress of thought would melt the isinglass.

I consumed everything, the fact of my being, the blackness of the bars, my self-imprisonment: no part was enough, only perfection was sustenance. The tigers were unescapable.

The keeper cackled, as I passed up and down, for he saw only the concrete and the animals.

'They will eat goats,' he said. And I laughed like a gong.

Perfection was a tantalus, a mystical tantalus. I strove in anguish, but I could never infer wherein it lay or whence it might be apprehended. Resistance entangled resistance in hard imagined approaches, and always there remained some ingress unexplored. I grew in depth and passion. Beyond the isinglass prowled the tigers. The adequate tigers. Life was magnificent. Every moment was magnificent.

I stretched into metaphysical causality, opposition and argument burned increasingly. The isinglass melted, slowly as a mountain wears away, and crept in folds down the public steps.

*

The sun was shining mellowly within the cage, and the bars were saplings of sweet-scented trees. They had taken root, and as I paused in my pacing, I saw vines creeping about them, green headed, hanging out their flowers and leaves.

'You must go to them,' the keeper said, 'to the yellow cats.'

I went slowly up the steps and pushed aside the bars. The steel retreated into vistas of sand, shimmering in a humid atmosphere. The smooth creatures, soberly streaked, enclosed me as I prowled about, licking my limbs with warm tongues, and swelling my beatitude with saccharic purrs. My body shone like almond blossom, beneath a tiger skin enclasped with gold.

*

The keeper strolled beside me on the concrete, rattling his keys, and calling to the animals. There was a rancid smell, and the cage was dark, with bars of rusted iron.

New English Weekly, vol. 3, no. 17, 10 August 1933, p. 396

Our modern Hesiod

Review of: *Collected leaflets of the Irish Free State Department of Agriculture*, 2nd edition, 1933

A volume an inch and a quarter thick, weighing two and a quarter pounds, with 784 pages of good, clear print and 106 illustrations, bound up in a businesslike manilla cover, and for sale, new off the press for one shilling, is worth examining further. There must be some reason why it is being sold at less than it cost to produce. The reason, here, is not far to seek: there has been a grant-in-aid from the Free State exchequer, and the motive: public instruction; for the betterment of the country's marketable produce, the suppression of disease in crops and animals, and the reduction of imports of feeding stuffs, fruit and the like, which could be grown within the country. The volume has a present political significance; it is also an excellent text-book of practical agriculture; but for the lay reader, it provides a book to read. It is not intended as such, and certainly not outside the Free State, but Saorstat Eireann would scarcely mind if a few discerning foreigners bought the volume, as they now can, from Easons in O'Connell Street, Dublin, by sending a shilling and the postage.

It is a rare bargain, but on turning over the pages the thought of having laid hands on a bargain dissolves and becomes trivial, for these collected leaflets are in truth a very bible of writings on the origins of human food and clothing, and the common occupations of the Irish people. They tell how to make a haystack, how to look after bulls, when to put lime on the land. They constitute no work of fiction, nor essaying, nor philosophy, and certainly nothing that will ever receive the commendation of the Book Society; but that which they have to impart ranks with the good hard-scrubbed furniture of the mind, matters of intranscendental fact, amongst which the imagination may dwell unsuffocated, at home on this earth, and through which the mind's eye can see the face of Ireland, even to the prevailing weather.

Regarded as literature, these leaflets have at least the merit of a clear and downright style; in matter they are homeric, pagan and strong.

The ears are cut off close to the skull.
The cheeks are separated from the face
by cutting and sawing through from the back
of the mouth on each side to just below
the ears and across the top of the tongue.
The tongue is cut off close to the lower jaw
and the latter cracked lengthwise to allow
the cheeks to lie flat, any traces of blood
being wiped off. The face, if it is to be cured,
is sawn or split lengthwise with a chopper
and the brains scrapped out.

Such detail, piled up, about so many human activities, conveys something of the grip and fun of life, no less than the smells and the cruelty. The sticking of pigs does not in the least affect the greenness of young corn. In concept, as in practical purpose, the whole work is in direct antagonism with the fogs of sentimentality and religious superstition. Thus for our serious moods, our moods of the morning, it is inspiring, it needs no translation. But when we are of a truffle-snuffling mind, it has succulencies rich as those of the Old Testament; terrors worse than antivivisection propaganda; quiet descriptions of evil, in words familiar and unfamiliar, that rival Poe and Baudelaire. Instance, the liver fluke of sheep, described as white leaf-like worms, whose eggs fall to the ground in the sheep's droppings, whence the larvae crawl into snails, whose bodies they eat, later to emerge and infest the grass, so passing again into sheep, to lay their eggs in the alimentary canal, and then bite their way through the intestines to the liver, where hundreds may be found, an inch long and half an inch wide, when the animal is dead. Such double parasitism is unparalleled outside the realm of literary criticism.

Twenty-four amongst these hundred and five leaflets concern disease, a consequence of the incessant strife between mankind and small pathogenic organisms for the food reserves of plants and animals. Shades of the potato famine, stacked histories of fear, emigration and the white forces of research lie tremulous behind Leaflet no.14, 'Potato blight and its prevention'. But turn a few pages and out comes this marvellous volume into the sun-shine again, with Leaflet no.8, again about pota-toes: the characteristics of the many varieties. The raising of new varieties of potato, and the identification, by small vegetative differences, of what is old, is one of the finest arts a man can give his mind to, a matter of exquisite per-ception, patience and unrecorded adventure.

But to peck such examples from so large a volume must be to give a distorted impression of it as a whole. To convey something of the air of enlightened peace, and the fascinating variety – not to say poetical juxtaposition, of the subject matter, it is better to enlist a few titles of the component leaflets:

> *The growing of oats. Defects of haymaking. The apple. Tuberculosis in poultry. The planting of waste lands. Swine fever. Potato culture on small farms. Advantages of early ploughing. Cow testing associations. Sea weed as manure. The use of home grown grain in the feeding of farm animals. Weeds. Home butter making. Marketing honey. Dishorning calves. Trees for shelter and ornament.*

No floundering here in the vapid responses of she-men to everlasting sexual insinuations: no pandering to sadism with the sensational; no pseudecclesiastic gas about Marxism. 'Have done,' say these leaflets: 'Damn spewing words about the varieties of your eroticism, let them complicate in your subconsciousness, if you have one, take them to bed with you, but come to work in the morning, there is still work to be done.'

Those whose spiritual progress has been out of the nihilism of War, through Lawrentian abandon into the waste land, and who still can see no hope, might take courage from these leaflets, in reflecting by how much we have already constricted certain malignancies of our erstwhile God, by violating the mysteries of some plagues and famines, and how, step by step, we are now advancing in quests of seem-ingly hopeless difficulty against virus disease. Agricultural research is generations in advance of our political and social development; even on the evidence of such work-a-day matters as its simultaneous investigation in neighbouring countries, its monthly abstracts of the world's literature on mycology and entomology, its one language of nomenclature, it has achieved a system of international communality, which is to our best, but near, ideal of Economic Nationalism, as Ely Cathedral is to a megalith. Over the hedges of our waste land it is good to contemplate Ely Cathedral.

But to return to these leaflets: if there is plenty in the world today, it has not been easily come by, and at a time when there is a tendency to take the fact of plenty for granted, it is salutary to read and learn with what dif-ficulty and sustained endeavour that relative measure of plenty is won. For it is ironical to speak of plenty to a generation that has had to adopt the mean expedient of birth control and deny itself children because children cannot be fed. There is plenty to supply the inadequate rations that are now endured, but when the crack comes, the resources of production will be strained, every nation must then look to itself, and the crack will come, for it is not the way of a genus that has mastered the earth to kill its children at the door of the womb for very long. The power of usury, the profit motive, the apathy and hysteria of incapable governments will be broken by that.

Although our crying immediate need is for the repair of the highways from production to consumption and the eviction of the toll-takers and gate-shutters along them, such heroic labour is not for all to undertake, and it is well that those who can increase the productivity of the land should stand firm to their posts. Their talents are required to maintain even that which we have. Their pres-ence, as manifested by these anonymous leaf-lets, is reassuring, for it means that when the call to other microscopes and scalpels is really heard, there will be no dearth of men who can grapple with reorganization as *they* now grapple with God and Death.

New English Weekly, vol.3, no.26, 12 October 1933, pp.608–10

Journey through Denmark

We were passing through intensely cultivated land, land that was being made not only to feed the country's population, but to provide a surplus to barter for tools and coal and steel; for Denmark has no coal or iron – practically no minerals at all. We missed the charm of our neglected countryside – for you cannot have it both ways; you cannot have a country heavily shaded with uneconomic trees; with great, wide, tangled coverts for pheasants in private estates; with the Highlands preserved for deer forests; with so much pasture – producing in meat only a fraction of the food value of the same area under cereals; and at the same time feed the population of the country. There is no countryside so delightful to wander about, or to regard from the windows of country residences, as that of rural England; its atmosphere, like the causes of its neglect, sentimental through and through – but we cannot afford this luxury of moods. We can no longer crowd our population into the black, intensive activities of industrial towns, and leave our countryside, pretty and wooded and half uncultivated, for the enjoyment of a privileged or discriminating few. Other nations are jealous of the sweets of industrialism, the mania for working in factories is world wide; we can no longer have a disproportionate amount of the world's coal mining and shipbuilding and cotton spinning to do. The Black Country is not going to be so black. We are not going to be allowed to do more than our share of the world's indoor, dirty work in our small country. There is a crack of light through our smoke-laden skies; soon we must plough up our half idle land or we shall starve. God in his infinite mercy is saving our people. *Life* will not be vanquished by *Death* – economic crisis, that is the name we give to the first insurgent wave of *Life*, breaking willy-nilly through the tight-drawn systems of death's forces, which we have been permitting under guise of our civilization. There is going to be an overthrow and an exodus.

But it would be hard to think that the English countryside must all become scratched up into little plots, a great allotment ground, dotted with Surbiton villas, like that part of Fyn, but that is stupid. It is not the necessity for growing food that builds houses cheap, quick and ugly; that is an urban influence. It is not the necessity for growing food that scratches up the land into little individual fields – that is a petty meanness of proprietorship, an expression of fear, a consequence of money idolatry, a beggar-my-neighbour pinking on the coffin lid of Death.

How, in nature, can the wide, free and unfenced reaches of corn, potatoes, mangolds, clover, in Jylland be less productive than these small holdings in Fyn? It is to Jylland that we should direct our eyes, for in Jylland much of the arable land has been reclaimed from waste, and that will be our problem too. I would not wish to walk over a fairer country than Jylland, with its great potato fields, its cooperatives and its grain. It is beautiful in appearance and function, and, with little of England's natural bounty of hills and rivers, its vistas give peace to the soul.

We came at last to Odense, the hub of main roads in Fyn, and the third largest town or City in Denmark. The order of importance being, we were told, Copenhagen in Sjaelland, Aarhus in Jylland, and Odense in Fyn. An ancient city, Odense, the city of Oden, and later, when the lightning of the old Gods persisted only in candle-glimmers and old tales, the birthplace of Hans Christian Andersen. A continental city, like others, but without the smell, absolutely without the smell; neither the German smell of boiling wurst and aborts, nor the French *soupçon* of drains. It was clean and fresh cooking; with a King's Garden for the unemployed to lounge in, and some old brickwork, including a cathedral dating back to the eleventh century, celebrating the murder of King Knud.

We were delighted to be in the town at first, for there is some magnetic influence along a main road which draws one to a big town, the allure increasing with the diminishing distance, as one approaches, according to the inverse square law; an allure that the relief of arriving seems at first to justify. We stared at the buildings, dodged the bicycles, which were there like a plague of weird ants amongst the vehicles, and ate Viennese cakes for tea. But in an hour we were tired, each new shop windowful of silver spoons, or tinted ladies' underclothing, more irritating than the last. We diverted ourselves for a time in trying to buy boracic lint – drawing sketches of blistered feet in respectable apothecaries', until the gentlemanly shop-assistants almost blushed and felt thoroughly uncomfortable, sending us off to drapers, perfumeries and furnishing ironmongers – anywhere, if we would only cease to lower the tone of their establishments. Boracic lint is not known in Odense; they use cotton and flannel. This trivial, not-particularly-funny-diversion played out, there was nothing for it but to go to the pictures. It always comes to that in big towns; although there is three times as animated a scene going on outside, all moving, all talking and all coloured. But it is too confused to contemplate and too strident to endure for long, without a grey lifelessness and fidgets coming over one. We did find a place showing a film made by a company in Copenhagen, but it did not disclose anything of the life of the Danes, or, for the matter of that, of any other people. Called a comedy, it was in fact a stringing together of all the conventional film skirmishes, supposed to represent the diffident approach of free individuals to self-abandon in the state of happy matrimony. Like most second-rate films its title should have been 'Through Vorlust to Coition'. There was also a jungle film. The jungle film makers have thrown over the last pretence of supposing that the public has any intelligence whatever; there is a terrible significance in the posters showing frail film actresses riding on the curved tusks of mammoths in full charge, or with their legs in the jaws of alligators. It means that the artists have thrown off pretence, and are gibbering at the public, playing balmy, trying to catch their thumbs with their fingers, and the public notices nothing that is not perfectly normal. 'Bring 'em back alive!'

We stayed that evening at a hotel where the band started playing at nine o'clock to a mysteriously empty restaurant, and where the people came in about eleven for drinks and dancing, which went on until two in the morning. By midnight there was a good rough house, with hefty raw-necked youths squeezing girls of very questionable virtue; twirling round or jigging up and down occasionally to keep up appearances. We saw the same thing elsewhere in Denmark, and it appeared to be the Danish idea of a popular dance: to pack the floor space as tightly as possible with clugging couples, then provide music and let them move en masse, as though they couldn't scratch their backs. It was there that we watched another type of Dane – the flighty waif, very soft and thin for her length, with a brightly painted face like the kind of boudoir doll that one gets for prizes at fashionable dances, and sits with legs dangling on dressing-tables. Very thin, seductive and poisonous probably, but even the fireships in Denmark are more respectable than their kind elsewhere.

We listened to the patter of bare feet up and down the landing in the middle of the night. At four o'clock someone banged on our door, furiously demanding Mathilde.

The next day, thanks to a suggestion from a friendly waiter who spoke German, we went to see the house where Hans Christian Andersen was born. The small rooms had been made to lead out of one another, for one way traffic, and the walls whitewashed for a picture gallery. There were manuscripts, autographs, Andersen's queer paper tearings and innumerable photographs. The great man seemed to have liked posing before the camera – that instrument having been invented that much too soon. It was disturbing to find him so like the film star, George Arliss. In one room his furniture and travelling bags, old silk hat, and even his death-bed had been collected, transhipped from America. The most significant exhibit by far the old leather travelling bags, which had become more and more solid with time and were then exhibiting their leather undisguised. In the back garden of the house the Municipality of Odense were busy erecting a futuristic mausoleum with mural decorations in commemoration of the poet. The colour of his stories ten thousand times diluted in paint.

Out to sea again, on the automobile ferry from Nyborg; we played hide and seek with the blue lobes of water between the corn when we were walking, and hide-and-seek with the pale land as we crossed from island to island. That morning the sea was a deep concentrated blue, black almost, and strong enough to be diluted twice for an ordinary sea. And the pale shores of Fyn lined it as far as the horizon as we curved out of Nyborg, the red and white flag of Denmark flying. There were smug moss patches of beech woods intercepting here and there the low yellow shore, and behind us the rapidly diminishing playbox town of Nyborg, with its green-spired old church, piled behind old brick buildings, and its new pill-boxes of oil tanks beside the harbour. The train ferries standing in their berths, high boxes built on ships, and looking like old white hens straining to lay eggs. Our ferry box was swollen as well, a great steel chamber within her, wide and tall and high, with hundreds of cars like a great modern garage. It was built in 1930 by the A-S Aalburg Maskin og Skibsbyggeri.

In mid-channel we passed a pale yellow sliver of an island, Sprogö, with two little dunes in its sand, a windmill, like a child's windmill on a stick, going round on one, and a tiny church on the other, and in between a red ark-like house. Not a real place at all, too pretty, too thin a sliver of sand to be out there all alone, in that troubled strong blue sea, but no doubt the gulls hump there in rows in bad weather, and one would find there goats and hens, and maybe patches of potatoes, besides the fishing nets hanging to dry.

There were two German youths on the ferry, one in black velvet corduroy jacket and shorts, the other in deep brown velvet; their flat bearskin packs lying on the deck with cooking pots attached; their shocks of hair flying about, a deep, intelligent, but wild, impudent and strong look in their sunbrowned faces.

Look out! ye sheep and idolators of this civilization, there are wolves amongst ye. Look to this generation in Russia and Germany, if your eyes are not too befuddled. There are those amongst them who have already learned all your tricks, who can play your games, and knowing you, have silently repudiated you and your values in their hearts. Your orders will change, for there is a power abroad mightier than your bankers and your guns. Look to a tansy growing, and you won't understand; look through your subsidized microscopes at a seedling lifting a stone, and you won't understand. Look at a bull calf just born, and you won't understand. Look to these young men everywhere abroad on foot about the land, and you won't see, you will never understand. But one by one surely, inevitably, you will lick death, and one by one, inevitably you will die.

Korsør, on Sjaelland, yet another white maritime town, brilliant in the sun, with masts, cranes and wharfside structures, like power at peace, showing through the buildings and at the blue end of the main street. Once more we walked straight by compass out of the town, on the last lap of our journey, once again prepared to find differences; so great a frontier is a belt of sea water. We walked across the place where the dust-carts tip their rubbish, eyeing the things that the townfolk had thrown away, for on such a walk as ours one sees everything, cathedrals, docks, farms, hovels, second-rate hotels, all – including the towns' dustheaps and the art galleries. Even in the dust heap there was a proper loop way for the carts, conscientiously made with old railway sleepers. Amongst the sour, garbage sodden paper, the bones and the ashes, we found a child's beheaded doll, with straw coming out, and deflated contraceptives that the towns-people had thrown away.

The fjord, called Korsør Nor, on the map, looked so alluring with its corn yellow shores meeting the blue water in a perfect line. We wanted to enter it, to come closer to it, and would have taken one of the white boats out on it, but the boatmen all said: 'Those boats belong to others, only this is mine.'

We tried then to reach the line of shore, where yellow met blue, but to do that was to search where the rainbow ends. The fenced properties reached down, barbed wire enclosed, to the last edge of the grass, and we could only pick our way over the narrow shelf between the grass and the water, where the wind had blown the dead papyrus of water weeds. Papyrus because the sun had bleached the upper surface of this flotsam paper white. In some places it lay on the shore like shavings, in others it was deep and wet, and black beneath the surface, decomposing with a smell more offensive than guano. The beauty of that water scene was to be experienced only with the eyes; we could not have it in any other way. To approach was to make it dissolve magnified away; we could not plunge within it, nor make its touch sentient, any more than a child may play with the children in picture-books. We went inland, gazing on that wonderful airy panorama of colours as it moved lazily past, fjord and whitewashed farm, cornrick and mangold field, in pace with our slow progression along the road. About us, as the road widened away from the water, was a countryside of windmills, willows and meres, with horses grazing on low pastures, and but for the high tones of light from the white buildings and that recessive fjord, an English scene. As we went on mile after mile, over the sharp flinted worn road, the pain of my blisters was very great, and my feet so inflamed that every step was a new agony. Hard luck to be cheated in this way, and have to limp along a mile an hour. But it was the penalty I had to pay for all those months of sitting about in offices, soft living, and driving that cheat of an all-destroying little car. For nearly a year I had not walked out far and straight on my own good feet over the country. No way of going has ever given me the deep, calm experiences of walking quietly over the ground amongst other living things: birds, beasts and flowers – I had given myself up too much to the way of life that society seeks to impose upon me. This walk from Esbjerg was a belated breakaway, a gesture of denial, an affirmation of belief in my inner knowledge of the good and the real; whilst the

voices in the purgatory of our modern civilization were saying: Why don't you take a little car? or go and stay at the Hotel d'Angleterre at Copenhagen and have a good time? or join a golf club? – walking like that on blistered feet is no holiday. Praise heaven! at least it was not that. *Holiday* – the reverse of the false coin, of which their *Work* was the blurred obverse. *Work*, which left me neither mentally stimulated nor physically tired.

The countryside of willows and meres gave way to a dull, wide stretch, with red houses vulgar upon it, like bungalows in Surrey, but that would not have mattered; we had already passed through the suburbs of Odense and the dust heaps of Korsør. The pain of my blisters, not the Danish jerry-builders, prevented me from going any further that day; and it was in sadness that we took a train from Svendstrup to Slagelse. As from an answering grace in the heart of things the train came up all snorting iron, black and unashamed, out of the late evening purple under a melon segment of moon, and the people in the bare wooden carriages were villagers going only a little way. A child lay limp, dead-whacked and abandoned to sleep in a woman's arms, falling on the floor like pliant rubber when they roused her at Slagelse.

We had only gone 14 kilometres by train; but I was tired and discouraged when we awoke the next morning in a shabby second-rate hotel, facing the station yard. Everything had suddenly gone flat. It seemed there would be nothing more in Sjaelland than walking over plains studded with bungalows and cut to pieces with well repaired fences and barbed wire; that every night we should eat lumps of steak, fried onions and half-boiled potatoes in Spisesals smelling of stale smoke and beer; that there would always be fur-coated prostitutes raucous in these eating rooms whilst the band played 'Kiss for kiss' and 'Who's my honey baby now?'; that everywhere we should find the dirty old Victorian coverlets of respectability warming the ghouls of self-indulgence. As I lay, late into the morning, looking through the grimy window curtains at the dull brickwork of the station frontage, it seemed that the familiar English urban atmosphere had again encompassed me; that my enthusiasm had gone out, and that spiritually our trek was done.

The old anxieties that lurked in my Killsblight occupations came back and rode me like evil hags. Why push on, to confer with those merchants in Copenhagen and be back in the works to time? Why not throw off my obligations into some blue fjord and be free? Why not go scribbling down there, by Langland and Laaland, Aero, Falster and Moen? There was no choice; I know not why. Some time perhaps I might come back and traverse those islands: always some other time, as though life went on for ever.

But that day, at last on foot again, through long, uninterrupted miles of beech woods on the way to Sorø, the calmness and merriness of my years came back to me again. There were again the wild deer leaping through the trees, and triangular piles of peeled pine spars, cut to length for pit props. We neither met nor spoke to anyone all day. At two o'clock, in a grassy clearing, we ate the smørrebrøt which we had bought from an automatic machine in Slagelse, liking the strong taste of the rye bread, and watching lizards turning on themselves and their moist quickness in the sun. In the late afternoon we crossed the Sorø Sø in a motor-boat, a great lake a mile wide and miles long, enclosed on every side by beech trees in unbroken surges of green, like a glass medallion pressed deep in a rug. The spell of depression had passed, and in the evening I noticed on a menu that 'forloren skilpadde' is Danish for mock turtle; and laughed as though there were nothing in the universe but one skildpadding mock turtle forloren amongst the stars.

In the morning: Sorø. With an academy corresponding to our Harrow or Eton, where the privileged youth of Denmark go for their disciplined lapping of the very best cream. A park town, with beech trees making shady avenues of the roads; the brickwork of the church, old buildings and gateways paled by a shade in eight or nine centuries, and now quietened with an ineffable patine, befitting the ideal and lovely antique culture playing over the male adolescents in the academy. The very beech trees coming down to the water, and the subdued regular ripples on the lake seemed accessory to the atmosphere, for in the morning light the Sorø Sø was a sophisticated great low park-water, dull as the representation of water on a steel engraving. Here and there about the town were ancient rune-stones, neatly placed, their antique writings like the word of Greek above a scholar's door. And in one ancient square there was a statue of some time-blackened old bourgeois hero holding out a scroll; too old and forgotten to have any significance remaining, or to make any disturbing philosophical challenge or political intrusion.

The Adelphi (new series), vol. 8, no. 6, September 1934, pp. 400–7

St Thomas De Quincey

Review of: Malcolm Elwin, *De Quincey*
(Duckworth)

There are good reasons why Thomas De Quincey should be of significant interest to this generation. The first, which concerns his Life, is that De Quincey was a man of great independence of spirit, a cultured pagan in a world of Christian pretension, who dedicated his life, at a very early age, to what he called his own 'intellectual development' – the cultivation of his own self-regarding faculties in a timeless flux of words – and who succeeded in pursuing his own way, from first to last, with an inspiring disregard of money, health, comfort and restrictive conventions. For us, whose lives are torn up with indecision and mixed aims, and whose best contemporary heroes, like the Lawrences, T. E. and D. H., have died frustrated men, De Quincey is very nearly a saint, and he is at least a hero in a world bloodthirsty for heroes. Consider his achievement: he set out to experience his own life – which for him involved the necessity of perfecting his own spoken and unspoken discourse. The means fused with the end, and the natural fruition of his endeavour was the writing of fine prose. In so far as this marked his success, he succeeded gloriously, and he succeeded by a subjective method and an introspective life mood, generally distasteful to the whole occidental world.

Mr Malcolm Elwin presents the main facts of De Quincey's life with fairness and sympathy. It is for the reader to penetrate the sympathy to get at the man. And does not each incident show De Quincey gently but steadfastly refusing to suffer fools gladly, to brook any deflection from his course? At sixteen he broke loose from his mother, who sought to maul piously over his spiritual being; ran away from a school at which he knew he was wasting his time; and found, in poverty and in the arms of the outcast Ann of Oxford Street, experiences of vital significance to him. He disregarded the honours that the University of Oxford had to bestow, and introduced himself at the age of twenty to Wordsworth and Coleridge. He took opium, regularly and irregularly, to enliven the play of his own consciousness and his enjoyment thereof; he slept with Margaret without bothering to ask Dorothy Wordsworth's permission, and married Margaret some three months after the birth of their first child; he wrote practically nothing during the first twenty years of his independent life, and when at last importuned by necessity to write for money, anatomized what the world regarded as a vice, flung his *Confessions of an opium eater*, which is three parts a blague, back at the world's head, without compliments, and took in exchange an immediate and lasting fame. He became the father of eight children, wrote enough prose to fill fourteen stoutish volumes in the selected edition alone, did a great deal of what is now called 'hiking' and travelling about the country in stage coaches, consumed, on his own uncorroborated *ipse dixit*, enough opium to poison several herds of wild elephants, and died at the ripe age of 74, still 'acknowledging nothing that calls for excuse'.

On the facts it would appear that the gentle De Quincey was a man of considerable virility and *esprit*. But unfortunately he was small in stature, suffered much from his stomach and had a real weakness for the society of 'cultivated' women. These circumstances, taken in conjunction with a very proper subconscious aversion to English Composition – with which De Quincey's prose is confused by educationalists – and with the story of his excesses, which De Quincey himself spread abroad so assiduously and which has been swallowed, hook, line and sinker, even to his alleged consumption at one period of no less than 1½ *pints* of laudanum per day, have given rise to the gentle degenerate legend, and to the habit of regarding De Quincey, always with great sympathy, as a sort of suffering little bookworm in petticoats for whom one must make excuses.

The present Life does not break away from the tradition. It is written with some detachment; it gives the factual aspects of the experiences over which De Quincey was for ever brooding, and it is enlivened with a number of charming anecdotes about the man, which may be interpreted according to taste. But withal it is too pleasant and reverential. It is neither analytical nor provocative, and does not therefore present De Quincey in the light of (God save the mark) our new dawn.

This is a pity, for De Quincey is a master, perhaps the greatest master that has ever lived, of the legato style of playing on the instrument of English prose. He is, in the Socratic sense of the word, a musician, and his kind of music is fast becoming a lost art. In this our time, when what passes for prose is syncopated, speeded up and made snappy with every device of appopocation and ellipsis, there is great reason why those who manipulate English should submit themselves to the cor-rective discipline of listening to the voice of De Quincey going on and on through the night. Considerable provocation is necessary to generalize this practice, since there is, it must be admitted, a great paucity of intellectual content in much of De Quincey's work. It is of no use reading snatches. For it is only when the reader has settled down to listen continu-ously, with impatience banished from his soul, that he will begin to come under the influence of De Quincey's slow, various and perfect phrasings, and be moved in grace, with De Quincey's hasteless regressive movement, over the extended consideration of trifling sentiments to magnificent appassionatas of deeply suffered experience. He must endure the 'mere instincts of revential demeanour' to savour the 'cancerous kisses of crocodiles'.

New English Weekly, vol. 8, no. 10, 19 December 1935, pp. 189–90

Hypnagogic hallucinations

Mr E.C. Large is by profession a chemical engineer and he is occupied in the development of new technical processes in industry. But, side by side with his activities in this direction, he has found time to develop a taste for writing which showed itself in his earliest years. His psychological studies, like the present one, are based on his own experiences. Eds.

Between the time of extinguishing the light and the time of passing into sleep we are not in total darkness. Although there may be no crack of daylight in the room and the eyelids are tightly closed, sensations of light persist. By a certain 'knack' or accident of attention these sensations can be distinguished as a succession of appearances of by no means feeble illumination.

There are, first of all, the *afterimages*, residual effects following the stimulation of the retina by light, which change in character as the excitation subsides. With my own eyes – and in what follows it is necessary to speak directly of personal experiences – I have repeatedly observed, for example, that after looking at the bright yellow filament of an electric lamp I perceive first a *positive* after-image, which is yellow and diffused, and which slowly con-tracts to a very small yellow image of the wire. Suddenly this changes to red, a *negative* after-image, which resembles a tiny, dull red, gridiron. This image in turn slowly fades and merges into the spangled, irregular grey illumi-nation which I can always perceive when my eyes are closed, in darkness.

If I then press upon my eyes, either with my fingers or by contracting the surrounding muscles, I induce other sensations of light: blue and greenish glows, which may be subdued, like the colours which appear in a film of heavy oil, or may quicken into soft flashes or rapidly changing areas. These are the *phosphenes*, fre-quently described in works on the physiological aspects of vision. They superimpose themselves over the grey meshes of my darkened field of vision, and change like the after-images, from positive to negative forms, usually from leaf-green to slate-blue and from slate-blue to leaf-green over the same areas.

In so far as these after-images, grey entoptic glimmerings and phosphenes are sensations of light occurring when no light in fact enters the eye, they may be regarded as optical illusions; but the imagination may be stirred, or may play, upon these faint sensations of light, giving rise to the next, and more interesting phenomena: hallucinations of form and colour in which appear likenesses of unconsciously remembered things. These latter appearances were first, named: *hallucinations hypnagogiques*, hallucinations on the threshold of sleep, by Alfred Maury in 1848. This is how Harvey de Saint Denis, 1871, describes such an appearance:

> A green hummock arose in the field before my inner eyes. I saw, more and more clearly, its masses of leaves. It burst and boiled over like a volcano, increasing and spreading with moving zones of lava. Red flowers issued from the crater in their turn and spread in an enormous bouquet. The movement stopped; the scene hung for a moment very clear, and then everything vanished.

But hypnagogic visions are not always so considerable as S. Denis's volcano. Often they are no more than patterns and simple likenesses of detached objects, occupying only a small portion of the field. I have seen the most complex images in the hypnagogic state, from gorgeous flights of tropical birds, to scenes in a laboratory, and an unforgettable spectacle of a child standing in a fire, and being slowly consumed in lambent flames; but of my own observations the following is more typical. I lay quiescent, with my eyes closed, listening to the distant sound of traffic. I saw nothing for a long time — save the grey entoptic glimmering, so familiar it appeared as nothing — when suddenly to the left of the field a tuft of quills, of a pearly white colour, emerged for a moment only. It was succeeded by a piece of jade, shaped to stand on a mantelpiece, and after that a plantation of self-luminous cabbages, each about as large and as tight as a football, arranged one at each corner of a rectangle, and one at the intersection of the diagonals – a quincunx of cabbages! And each image so clear it would seem the easiest thing in the world to draw or paint it on paper.

Dr Eugène Leroy, in a recent little book, uniquely devoted to the description and interpretation of these phenomena (*Les visions du demi-sommeil*, Librairie Félix Alcan, Paris 1926) has collected a great many descriptions and even pictorial representations of the appearances from a number of trustworthy observers. They range from simple geometrical forms, and star-like constellations, to scenes of considerable elaboration, but the vividness and clarity of the description is always such as to indicate a like vividness and clarity in the appearances themselves: as though, before projection in the hypnagogic field, they had passed through a psychical process of clarification leaving only significant essentials.

Any scene or object constantly present and viewed incidentally during the day tends to reappear amongst the hypnagogic visions. Thus an angler may see the likeness of moving weeds or ripples on the surface of water, and the appearances may often be traced back to their original stimuli in waking consciousness. But the eye appears to exercise a selection of its own amongst the stimuli which shall affect it. I have had the curiosity to stare fifty times a day at a certain plaster figure, in the hope of inducing the appearance of some likeness of it in the hypnagogic state, but without the least success: whilst the act of sawing a small branch from a pine tree, of which I took no particular notice, and which occupied me for at the most ten minutes, served to fix the appearance of pine needles so firmly in my sensory organism that I saw them hypnagogically every evening for a week afterwards.

This is not the only instance in which green objects, particularly growing parts of plants, have shown a propensity to reappear on my hypnagogic scene, and as these appearances have not coincided with any special interest on my part in either horticulture or botany, I have speculated on the reason for it. The phosphenes produced in my eyes are, as I have said, usually slate-blue or leaf-green in colour, and this latter hue, occurring in a particular area of vision, is very frequently succeeded by the appearance of a bud or other vegetative form. It is significant that green light is predominant in the solar spectrum; and that this light is rejected from all the green vegetation of the earth; but it would be fool-hardy to suggest that this tendency of green light to promote hypnagogic appearances has any universality.

I have tried to bring about the reappear-ance of an object, other than green in colour, not by staring at it during the day, and thus perhaps defeating perception by an alien process of concentration, but by working upon the object with active interest. I chose a piece of hard, white wood and, walking about the fields for many hours, carved it, with a penknife, into the nearest approximation to a sphere that I could manage. The little ball was vivid in the sunlight, but it was not reproduced amongst that evening's succession of visions: patterns of leaves appeared and a tortoise that I had forgotten having seen, but nothing of the ball.

Alfred Maury, approaching the study of dreams through that of hypnagogic hallucina-tions (*Le sommeil et les rêves*, 1861) laid the foundation for the rational appreciation of the dream – in terms of objective science – as a phase of human experience. This way of appreciation (followed in recent times by Yves Delage – *Le rêve*, 1919) is essentially syn-thetic, contemplative and formative, and is in direct opposition to the subjective and ideol-ogy-ridden methods of Freud. It is of interest to revert to the relationship, perceived by Maury, between the hypnagogic hallucination and the dream. In the hypnagogic state we are observers, we lie relaxed, and so long as we maintain the necessary uninquisitive mental attitude, and observe without looking too hard, the self-evolving imagery goes on, like a spectacle in a theatre. We are so far awake that we may even describe it, in carefully cho-sen words, to another person in the room. With the oncoming of sleep the succession of images continues, but our awareness passes

to a further remove of self-identification and quiescence, the observational plane vanishes, and we leap down on a stage, where unfatigued resources of memory provide not spectacle but adventure.

It is sometimes possible to trace the components of a remembered scrap of dream back through hypnagogic appearances to events in waking consciousness. Thus: I once dreamed that I was cast into prison and tor-tured in an Iron Maiden. My mode of escape and my complacent explanation of it belonged entirely to the province of the dream: the spikes entered my body but could not harm me because I was *spiritual*. But the Iron Maiden was in imagic succession with a pair of boots, that I had observed in the hypnagogic state: boots that had long upstanding nails and were hinged down one side like shell fish. And these in turn were clearly related to a solid pair of boots, into whose soles I had actually driven climbing nails the day previously.

Hypnagogic hallucinations tend to be more numerous and perhaps more vivid than usual when one is in a feverish or nervously excited state, when the neural mechanism of vision is disturbed; it is recorded that it is in such circumstances that the appearances have first forced themselves upon the attention of persons not previously given to observing them. When, for example, during an attack of influenza, scene after forgotten scene in the countryside drifts within the closed eyes as though projected by green light from a cinema photographic film. But the undisturbed, soft, and often beautiful succession of these images, which occurs in normal health at the threshold of sleep, is as natural as the song of birds or the drifting of clouds across the sky.

There has been much controversy whether these hypnagogic appearances should properly be considered hallucinations or illusions. Within the terms of reference of physical science it is ultimately an exceedingly fine issue, and the keen instrument of French prose has been used to divide the single hair of distinction lengthwise into a multiplicity of parts. The favoured explanation appears to be that the mere shapes and movements of entoptic light, the 'illusion' of light due to electrical or pressure excitation of the retina, suggest patterns of things to the half-conscious mind, and that these imaginings are then projected back as an optical hallucination. Alfred Maury's pronouncement is that the visions have as substratum an illusion and it is only when the mental disturbance is complete that the hallucination appears, apparently spontaneously.

Whatever the scientific definition, the visions remain, a universal, but infrequently considered part of human experience. Their role in the psycho-physical mechanism of human creativeness – by whatever force that functioning may be inspired – has received all too little consideration in the literature of the West. Chiron, the Phoenix and Siva of the Seven Arms have visual forms that may well have been first fixed so significantly, from depth associations in the field of *les visions du demi-sommeil*.

The Aryan Path, vol. 7, no. 7, July 1936, pp. 305–8

The Stour Valley

The winter is breaking up; the sun has passed the equinox, and there it is now, above me in the blue hemisphere, in magnificent combat with the clouds. It penetrates their fringes with a glorious radiance, angrily and insistently they drift past it in their masses, striving for domination of the sky. The earth is dark, the wind is cold and charged with snow. The clouds disperse, they tear apart and once again the sun bursts through, its radiant warmth instantly penetrates the cold air, an area of light moves over the tilled fields. Once again I am walking alone in the first days of spring. Whilst my friends engage in disputation and there is carnage in Spain, I shall walk from Ely to Colchester.

So this: this little grass-banked channel, not six yards wide, is Soham Lode. Its bank burst at Barham and flooded a few fields; from the reports in the newspapers it might have been the Mississippi. The Floods! The Fens under Flood! All night vigils in the Fens! Homes in Peril! It is true that the Ouse is swollen, at Ely it has covered the wash-lands, many hundreds of acres are indeed under water and reflecting the sky, but where are the houses submerged and where are the families migrating from their homes? That puff of inky exaggeration is far away now, it lingers in London; it belongs there, like the murky squalor of Liverpool Street Station. Here the yellow chaffinches forage over the newly upturned black soil, the straw ricks are dry, and the rows of old cottages abut at all angles to the skyline and the roads, dry as baked clay.

Aeroplanes pass overhead, they have become as familiar as the birds, but a stranger pacing along the road with a rucksack on his back makes a momentary disturbance in the brooding life of the country people. Children gather together and stare blankly after me as I pass, and old folk watch me out of the corners of their eyes and whisper together.

The Crown Hotel, Newmarket, very dingy outside but with an old yard not much altered since the last coach drew out of it:

'Got a room?'

'Aad! Genulmun wansa room!'

'How much: bed and breakfast?'

'Six an' six.'

'Can I have some tea?'

'Wotcherwant?'

The thin woman in the apron disappears grumbling at Aad, and Aad, in the bar, continues to hum as she looks out of the window. I sit on one of the settles in the bar parlour and watch the firelight playing over prints of classic racehorses, with long chisel necks. I have to wait for my tea only so long as it takes to put eggs and bacon in a pan and fry them. This is a good place, unpretentious, and there's no sham politeness and servility. I have walked from Ely without a halt and my legs ache. For the last few miles I avoided thinking about them by reading Alexandra David-Neel on Mystics and Magicians in Tibet. They use meditation as an anaesthetic when their bodies begin to putrefy, and when a man dies the Lamas assist his spirit to escape – through a small hole in the top of his head – by sitting round him and shouting 'Hik!' with the necessary extrusive force. It takes a period of intense silent concentration to work up sufficient power and they bring up the syllable at last from the depths of their bowels, afterwards spitting blood.

I feel extraordinarily content to sit in this bar parlour, making a couple of pints of beer last me all evening and talking as well as I can to those who come in. The difference between them and me is that they speak spontaneously, never heeding or seeking their words, whilst I have to rehearse everything beforehand, casting it into their idiom as best I can. When I have said anything I listen to see whether it will pass. I manage fairly well, even getting away with a couple of little stories and making them laugh, which I regard as a triumph. At least I have not cast over their good company the cold suspicious blight which greets the intrusion of a 'gentleman'. They understand cyclists, and by the end of the evening I have almost convinced them that in walking across the country I am only a cyclist without a bicycle, and not necessarily a suspicious character. It isn't so bad, when you go walking with a girl, because everybody knows what you go walking with a girl for, but walking alone, it really is very queer.

A rubicund friend of the 'management' comes in with his wife. They are both passing stout and saggy about the eyes; they tell me how they once used to go to Yarmouth in a pony trap or waggonnette, and how they always used to give the horse a pint of beer with a sop of bread in it, at Newmarket. The beer was twopence a pint then. Presently a friend of theirs, Maudy, comes and sits at the table. She is twenty-five, tough, powerful and very good-looking. She is a barmaid, and I reckon it would take a pretty hefty and equally vital young man to play Romeo to her. She is lively and has plenty of oil in her lamps. She talks about men: '... he'd come a-running after me, soon enough, if I wanted him, but he's messing about and making nothing of his life.' To how many of the cultivated white rats of my acquaintance would not that apply? She has more poise, more knowledge of life and of the world, and more character than any ten of the silly trollops who live in Hampstead and gas about psychology. I warm myself in her presence, she provokes in me a certain secretive warmth of carnal desire, but I am comfortably conscious that I don't want her. But I can talk to her as to an equal, for after some of the things I've done to earn money, I'm just about on a level with any barmaid alive.

Good Friday, and a cold bright morning. The snow lingers on the leeward side of piles of stones by the road. Racehorses are being exercised on the slopes, a great many of them. Newmarket is the headquarters of horse-racing in England, and the town is a little oasis of prosperity. There are many stud stables on the Downs and the estates are trim and well-kept. With the Towers at Kirtling the parson's pleasure country, which is the valley of the Stour, really begins. Alternating sweeps of brown tillage and sheep's pasture bear down gently to a little depression in the land which marks the course of the young river. They are wide and long, these fields, and marked by occasional rows of elms, with here and there a rectory or a hall or a farm, or an ancient square-towered church, always half concealed by the elms. The most active inhabitants of this country are the rooks, for the higher branches of the elm trees are black with their nests, and the birds put up an incessant clamour. There are very few footpaths, for the land is most genteelly private and enclosed, but from Kirtling to Great Bradley I found one, three miles over the grazing. To walk there is to be at the centre of a blue hemisphere, with the land vacantly green, a lonely spectator of the clouds. There are black cattle and flocks of earth-stained sheep; the blackthorn hedges have not a leaf nor a flower upon them; the small birds scurry along the ditches but there are only last year's nests.

At Great Bradley I cross the Stour, it is there no more than a brook that it would be easy enough to jump over, were it not for the overhanging willows. I go on through Thurlow and Great Wratting and Kedington. Once I stopped for bread and cheese at a pub where there was a blind man. The bar was cold and they were burning eggshells and kitchen scrap on the smoky fire. Besides the smell there was something indefinably worn and vitiated in the atmosphere, a lowering of tone, a lack of vitality. And then I knew it was because of the blind man. It is harsh and sad, but it is true that physical deformity or deficiency lowers the vital tone of all life in its neighbourhood, a taint is to be felt from the walls and the floor and the very air, wherever an idiot, or a blind man, or a cripple dwells. Blind men often grow stout, they feel their way with their feet, walk with their heads up, never looking down, their sightless eyes staring straight before them, their faces dead and expressionless. They can never perceive a smile nor answer it. Death walks with a blind man.

I left my lunch uneaten and walked on, conscious that I was counting the miles. Kedington: an untidy, sprawling village, with many jerry-built bungalows, and allotments, and an Institution there, of some kind; the

Risborough Home, seeming to drain the vitality and lower the vital tone of the village exactly as the blind man had done at the pub. A mill by the river now, and already water enough for that. It begins to snow, and in an hour the day has changed from the bright beginnings of spring to the depths of winter. The snow in great flocks swirls about me as I leave the river and take the most direct road to Clare. It is very beautiful, the snow, and the patterns of its motion as I see them, relative to my own. Gravity draws the flakes down, the wind blows them across, and my advance causes them to approach me. I forget that I am hungry and that my feet are tight in my shoes, lost in the sheer pleasure of watching the three-dimensional movement of the falling snow. Soon it covers the entire landscape and the trees are loaded with it on one side and black on the other.

I come to Clare at five in the afternoon; it is cold, every door is shut, nobody is about; it is like a village of the dead. The great old church, big enough for a cathedral, blocks the long street, but there is no sign of a hotel, and I cannot walk on another ten miles to Sudbury. Passing round the church I find the welcome word 'Hotel' in faded paint on a wall. It is the 'Bell.' But it is all shut up, I ring for ten minutes and nobody answers; I limp on and come to another, but again it is shut and nobody answers. At last I find an inn where the door is open, and can sit down in a dingy little parlour where an oil-stove gives little warmth but much smell. There is a family having tea, they have come from London by car to see the church. I sit shivering with wet feet and listen to their witless conversation. 'A stitch in time saves nine', says the mother to one of the girls who is making a fuss about a ladder in her stocking, and they all laugh, and look across at me, as though to draw me into appreciation of the joke.

When they have gone I ask the maid why anybody ever comes to Clare; she says it is a very old town: there is the church, and a priory with ruins, inhabited by one Lady May. She is sure I have only to ask and Lady May's gardener would permit me to go over the grounds. Sir Henry May's ashes are scattered there, and there is the Tomb of Joan of Acre. Oh! it is a most interesting town, university people from Cambridge come to look at it, and there is supposed to be an underground passage from the priory to the church. There had even been a book written about it, by a local resident, she'd get it for me.

There is a bit of a fire in another room, and a tall young man, an hypochondriac, sitting in the dark. He says he will be better later when the bar opens and he can get a drink; it will ease the pain in his chest and he will be able to play dominoes; in Clare one has to do something to pass the time or one would go mad. I sit there in the dark with him for an hour, because there is no other fire, but shrinking into myself all the time, and breathing through my nose because I think he has consumption. I go into the bar as soon as it opens, but it is mean and cold and the people are all worn or sick or tired. I watch them playing dominoes and drinking beer to kill time. When I next feel a romantic yearning to live in the country I shall remember this bar. In the country there is not only the sun and the fresh air. There is also the cold and the wet. These people are the human wash of the cold and the wet; life on the soil does not only give strength, it breeds consumptives and half-wits and rheumatics also. The cottages, so pleasant to look at on a summer day, there is not one of them that does not house something of a dull, enduring misery which haunts the countryside.

It cannot be said that nothing ever happens at Clare; this afternoon one of the tarred windmills over by Bures caught fire and went up in a blaze, and there was an accident on the road. A large car, driving through the snow, ran into the local doctor as he came out of a gate in his Austin Seven. The Austin Seven was knocked over on its side and the doctor popped up through one of the windows inquiring whether anybody was hurt. And even this evening there is something doing, the local incumbent has a Special Service for Men, and they tell me there is sure to be plenty of room for me, as the usual congregation is only about five. I prefer to read the History of Clare,

by G. A. Thornton, the local resident. It was published by Heffers in 1928. It is certainly interesting, with much good matter about the Austin Friars, and the life and troubles of the clothmakers who were established at Clare in the fifteenth and sixteenth centuries. Much also about 'says' and 'bays', the kinds of cloth they made.

In the morning Clare has a mild and peaceful beauty, it has arisen from the catalepsy of Good Friday, the shops are open and people are about. The river Stour has become as wide as Beverley Brook where it joins the Thames, and goes winding on through its double line of willows. But the quiet Suffolk grace of this countryside, that is so much the beauty of the clouds and the play of sunshine, serves but to lend poignancy to an ever-present sense of decay. There are many comfortable livings endowed in perpetuity by ancient families, but their incumbents preach in churches which are nearly empty. The halls are many of them still occupied, but the local gentry have no longer any real responsibilities in the rural life. They are impoverished and have only just enough themselves to keep their walls and fences and barbed wire in repair. The agricultural workers are poor; the villages remain as they have been for hundreds of years. There are good farms, but they are little more numerous than the rectories and the halls, and much of the land is being put to no use, except for summer grazing. O! it is very fair country, but it lies sleeping, it awaits a new surge, a new lease of human life upon it. It awaits the strong act of possession, the occupancy and use of a sturdy and no longer faded human population who have the will and the desire to work it and give it fecundity. It belongs now to the frogs, the parsons and the rooks.

In the water meadows by the now widening river there are places where the frogs are spawning. Brown water holes amongst the reeds where the masses of spawn are floating, and down below, the frogs, many of them together, the females swollen and lying immobile, whilst the males claw over them or drift exhausted. And the rooks disturb the sleep of the dead from the tree-tops above the churchyards, contumacious and eager, pairing and rebuilding their nests. The currant bushes are in flower, there are a few hazel catkins and willow pussies in the hedges, but as yet no leaves. The inconspicuous green dog's mercury is in flower, the goose grass is beginning to crawl up the banks, in the gardens there are a few daffodils. It is the Black Spring. Soon now the green will burst in its accomplished tender glory over the whole countryside, as yet, it is the Black Spring.

Cavendish. A genteel village with a fine green, above which stands the church, with a white ensign flying, and yellow houses, gabled and thatched. The river divides because of the mill, there is an island, and the tailrace rejoins the stream. Foxearth. Such a hamlet as the name implies: mud and duckponds, and cattle-trodden yards beside the road, and once again I am crossing the Stour. It is thirty yards wide now. This is the Constable country, though Constable's favourite haunt was further down, by Dedham nearer the sea. But Constable set himself before these scenes in high summer, catching the subtleties of the sky's light in con-flict with the sombre and deeply enshadowed lush of terrestrial green. Today the light is sharper, the trees are in silhouette, the sky is more frank, the earth is unembarrassed by richness of colour; the scene is gayer and there are bolder contrasts of meadow and arable land.

I trespass over the water meadows on the way to Sudbury, and rest on some old tim-bering above a weir, wondering if that water-mill works or whether it is not yet another relic of a past age, a picturesque obstruction of the river. While I am trespassing I come to a place where a plane tree has cast its leaves. They lie about it, undisturbed from last year and by some accident of the damp they have rotted strangely, all the flesh has gone but the veins remain, bleached skeletons of perfect leaves, delicate as lace.

Sudbury. A long approach to it through streets of suburban houses. It is a fair-sized town, not unlike Colchester, and it has two cinemas and a bus centre. Gainsborough lived here: fancy tea-shops and warming pan

emporiums bear his name. But Sudbury has a bit of a market, many shops and is a busy town. It stands on a hill, with the Stour below, assuredly a river now and rather like the Cam. I got to a children's matinee at one of the cinemas; it is packed with children and the management really know what they like. They roar with applause for the athletic heroes and hiss the slimy villains, they stand on the seats and yell for Laurel and Hardy and are not nearly so much interested in the exploits of 'Our Gang'. A pity the programme has been chosen so well, for I should like to hear their reception of that nasty little precocity, Shirley Temple, of any consciously 'educational' film, and of Disney's sophisticated extravanganzas.

They say it is ten miles by river from Sudbury to Bures – which is pronounced 'Bou-is' – and only six by road. The valley widens here, it is a couple of miles between the higher ground on either side, and the river winds tortuously through a strip of green meadows that it has made its own. It asserts the right to them by flooding them occasion-ally. A fine stretch for boating in the summer. A cluster of cottages round a narrow zigzag road, the windows yellow tablets where the oil lamps are already lit. Bures. And not much sign of an inn. But the harder a lodging is to find the less commonplace it is likely to be, that is why I did not stay in Sudbury. At the 'Eight Bells', when I pushed hesitatingly at the door somebody called to me to come in and make myself comfortable by the fire. Cheerful and goodnatured people here, and their way of saying the evening is cold is to remark that 'it 'ud be a bit nippy for Charley if he went out without his trousers'. The village cynic, who has stopped for a pint on his way home with some rabbits, reckons it was all wrong that the flying boat Copernicus should have crashed – a perfect piece of machinery like that, with all that high-class science could give it, to go and crash into a mountain – it wasn't right somehow: a thing that should not happen, like a back wheel coming off a Rolls Royce. I sug-gest it was an act of God. Like the misfortune of the family in Kent who woke up to find their back garden had disappeared into the earth, leaving a deep hole. That was an act of God. Most catastrophes are acts of God. But when there is a bumper harvest or a good herring catch, nobody says that is an act of God. He gets all the blame but no thanks, which is not altogether fair. 'Ah, now,' says the one with the rabbits, 'we are getting on to deep subjects. Our parson hasn't got much to do, but mind you, we respect him, I say nothing against parson or the old gentleman.' Aye! that's right enough, say the others. So we change the subject: where am I likely to find a lodging?

From the 'One Bell,' up by the dyeworks, there is a sound of singing and mouth-organs, like a pub by the docks. I go in by the saloon door, rather diffidently, and have to bawl to the landlady through the din, to know if she has got a room. She bawls back that she has, and that it will be quieter presently. I sit in the saloon bar with my beer, but gradually I become aware that there is something very fine about the singing next door, it draws me, and presently I take my glass in there, on the pretence that I need to buy cigarettes. Two brothers, both hefty Irish sailors, are leading the singing and varying their contributions with step dances and obbligatos on the mouth-organ. Everybody in the bar is singing, strong men's voices, and I find it good to join in, my own voice hitting into the vibrant wall and crash of sound. This is no singing to a drawing-room piano, no singing to gratify the pretensions of people who can't sing themselves: it is the direct outburst of men's voices when they can and do sing. To sing to raise the roof, not caring a damn for anybody, lost in the pleasure of singing for its own muscular sake, to be solid, and for once in total accord with a room-full of fellow human beings: it is a rare experience. Life seems to break at last through the commonplace, the confinement of one's own tincan individuality is raptured. When the singing has got to that point, it does not matter who buys the drinks, an empty glass is then just a 'dead man' for the nearest to fill. It does not matter what we sang,'When you grow too old to dream', 'Tipperary', 'Tickle me, Timothy', 'When Irish eyes are smiling',

it is good, it is very good; and something that no man could order, or contrive, or *buy*.

I go out into the road after the last song and walk about the village. There is a full moon over the house-tops and the shapes of the houses are deep and mysterious. The world for me has come alive again, as, when I started on this tramp I secretly hoped and secretly knew that it would. Be it noted I thank no woman for this, and it is not the beer. I could take four times as much as I have had tonight and find only self-hatred and nausea. In part it is the effect of walking fifty miles, perhaps the cleansing effect of moderate physical fatigue, I do not know.

I slept soundly last night and I awake to the virginal freshness of another spring day; to the cool, sweet air of the countryside, to its tremulous, aerial sounds. My breakfast is laid for me by an open window and there is new bread.

The Adelphi (new series), vol.14, no.2, November 1937, pp.50–8

Ten thousand faces

It is an eerie and a horrible experience to be in attendance on a stand at a Flower Show, day after day, and to watch the staring faces that come to rest before my exhibits and then move on. From right to left, from left to right they pass, these faces, propelled with hesitating pace and starkly turned towards me. I watch them, because I cannot help but do so, and in the day's reckoning I have looked into perhaps five, perhaps ten thousand human faces.

I do not watch, I search these faces, for mask-like as they are, they are not masks, but sensitive flesh in which the secrets of humanity are deeply chiselled for him who can to read. I am continuously searching the faces, and this close attention, and the repeated stimulation of one kind of cerebral activity, brings on sleep. I struggle with a great sleep that yawns to engulf me. What I see in the faces is incommunicable; but it promotes the release of ideas, with which I play, and by which I manage to hold myself awake.

To observe faces, as I am doing from the interior of this stand, is like observing birds from a hide. No one notices the quiet regard of my eyes, nor even, latterly, the tiny lens of the camera, behind a hole in the staging, with which from time to time I honour these faces with a record, when they stop transfixed before my bait – a model of a caterpillar feed-ing on a leaf. They do not know, these victims of mine, that that smirk or that intentness, that silly giggle, or that affected horror with which they respond to my stimuli, will emerge later, in the bowels of my cellar, ectoplastically, as a permanent image in silver. There is a streak of cruelty in Science.

I am no anthropologist, but it seems very strange to me that anthropologists should always be hiking away to the Caucasus, Mongolia, or the Polynesian Islands to look for material, when for the smallest of fees, any one of them could come here and share my hide. Perhaps anthropologists do not work here

for precisely the same reason that not one of my victims has so far seen the little lens of my camera; they do not see things which are immediately in front of their noses. They need red or yellow skins, or decorative weals on the bodies of savages to advertise to them the presence of their material. No one will see my camera unless I hang a notice, 'This is a Camera' beside it, and even so not one in a hundred would twig for what private purpose it is being used. That is my first observation about these faces, and they have eyes which do not observe unadvertised phenomena.

My next is that these faces all appear set to confront something that is not, in fact, before them. Their expressions are those of reticence, defiance, assumed indifference or bravado, they are all up against something that just is not there. It is not only the necessity to keeping awake by conscious effort, which comes over everybody in museums and shows, it is, I suppose, some one or other of the multitudinous aspects of the Devil, projected in their souls, and appearing to them, beyond sight, as an evil that retreats before them. These faces of clever jacks set to say 'You can't teach me'; the phlegmatic dials of heavy middle-aged men, the decorated features of would-be coquettes in garish hats; the sharp suspicious ferret eyes of small middle-aged ladies; the fat smirks of salesmen – 'My bubble won't burst'; the set composure of married women; the critical poise of the intelligent, who allow themselves sometimes to be amused – confident that no harm can come of it; the tusky insolence of elderly clerks … these faces, these anxious, ingenuous, vapid, independent, shy, belligerent, clever-pained, smirking, bitter, brave or hateful faces, they have all one thing in common, they are advancing in face of a phantom enemy.

I feel no sympathy, liking or dislike for these faces. I am aware that my own is but another of them, that my own melancholy and resentful countenance is surely enough repuls-ing its own phantom Devil; but because of that I do not experience any sentiment of kindred with the faces, or with the people of whom they are part. I assume that I shall never see them again, and they might be made of *papier mâché* for all I care. It is true that now and then somebody steps up and shakes me warmly by the hand, remembering some conversation at another Show, but I have invariably forgotten his face. He talks for a while and then bears off to right or left and vanishes.

Of course I have business to do. All these faces are of prospective customers. I am here and the whole stand is designed for the one purpose of associating the names of our stuff with their ideas about the maladies of plants. We want to make them think of us. So it is my duty to seem pleasant, and to give away information, to empty out a bottomless cornu-copia of information, sugared with every kind of helpfulness and inducement to buy. Heaven knows I do my duty. But all this smiling and talking is but a movement in the bass, a running accompaniment to the horrible procession of faces.

When there is a lull, and for a minute or two a gap in the stream of people, their faces do not desert me; memories and anticipations of them move across my mind, provoking questions, endless questions, but not questions of mycology. I wonder what worlds, or what strange refractions of perhaps but one world, exist beyond those thousands of pairs of eyes. Even in this little pursuit of horticulture, which seems so petty and so truncated to me, I am convinced that there is to be found much pleasure, that these people or many of them enjoy: delights to which I am numb. They see beauty in the colourful reproductive organs of plants, cut off and massed leaflessly on seeds-men's stands. For them, gardens populated with vegetative abortions, with all the awful results of plant surgery, isolation and goose-liver fattening with heat and fertilizers, have a kind of dream beauty. No! not dream beauty, I will not misuse words. They have for the horticulturalists the particular beauty of their particular heaven. A very different thing. I do not sympathize, I do not understand. I can in some measure perceive the functional beauty of plant growth, the beautiful unity of a plant organism, and also, shall we say, Goethe's

concept of a plant. I like the cow parsley that grows in our hedges, and am sorry to see it cut down with a scythe. I have greatly enjoyed making little ecological surveys on heaths and meadows, lying in the sun and counting the many kinds of plants enclosed within my square of tape, speculating on their struggle for space and sunshine. But these people, these horti-culturalists, for whom I make chemicals, take pleasure in grass lawns, and their nice green is a bleeding shambles of crippled and stunted plants. These people and I are wide as the stars apart. I see only the surface of their faces.

This lady to whom I have last been speak-ing, if I told her what I have just written, she would not think it could be true, she would stare at me in amazement or think me insane. And yet she has solemnly informed me that caterpillars lay eggs, she is proud of herself for having cut down a hazel copse to make a garden with herbaceous borders, and at this moment she is over at the stand opposite buying herself the latest novelty in chromium plated spades. I do not say she is insane, I do not even think so, I am just sorry I do not understand. They are remote, these faces, remote from me as the whole meaning and reason of the Horticulture at which they come to stare.

New English Weekly, vol. 12, no. 1,
14 October 1937, pp. 9–10

Children on the Mappin Terrace[1]

Joint review of: C.W. Kimmins, *Children's dreams* and Marjorie Thorburn, *Child at play* (George Allen & Unwin)

Since Dr Marie Stopes introduced Charing Cross Road to the middle classes there has grown up amongst us a somewhat peculiar attitude towards children. We consider our economic circumstances when preparing for bed. It is all very hygienic and prudent, but when we do decide that we can afford a child, or another child, we tend to expect from it full value for money. We see the child more as a very expensive Angora rabbit with charming tricks than as a human being. Somehow it isn't quite like ourselves; we make an extraordinary fuss about it, we are proud of having afforded anything so dear, and we *observe* it. All its little ways.

Very often, and indeed usually, we do love our children: that, like the course of their growth within the womb is something we can't alter. But superimposed upon that love, and all too often in the name of it, we do something which we like to call child-observation or child-psychology. In other words we stare at the child, and we are concerned to provide it with the right environment – to put it on a really well designed Mappin Terrace. We also talk a great deal about these acquisitions of ours; and popularized psychology, with its imposing cant terms, provides ready-made ideas for millions of earnestly conversational mothers and fathers.

Whilst entering into this game – with qualified enthusiasm – we may at least insist that if children are to be made the subject of psychological *experiments*, then the experiments should be good, with conditions reasonably devised to bring out the information desired. Dr C.W. Kimmins, a retired chief

1. The Mappin Terraces are an artificial mountain landscape at London Zoo, built for bears and similar animals. [RK]

inspector of LCC schools, purports to inform us about children's dreams. This is interesting, as the most pertinacious of parents find the child's dream difficult to 'explore'. We wonder how Dr Kimmins got his authentic dream material. Nothing could be more simple; a large number of children of various age groups, in LCC, secondary and reform schools, were just given, as a surprise subject for their weekly composition, the writing of a true and full account of the last dream they could remember; and the experiment had an added interest as it was made towards the end of 1914–18 war period.

The lack of imagination and emotional content in these children's 'dreams' would be incredible, if we did not take into account the conditions of the experiment. All these essays were written some time after the alleged dreams, and by school children in class, afraid to put down anything that teacher might think ridiculous or silly. Such conditions clearly tend to favour the stodgy children who write what is unexceptionable and common-place, and to silence the more sensitive, who can to some extent remember their dreams, but for whom they mean something much too mysterious to recount to anybody who has not their closest love and confidence.

Throughout this book there is no sign of any awareness that the child has a rich inner life of its own, of which only hints are revealed to the adult, and only then if he or she can listen very humbly. But pedagogues never realize that school education destroys as much as it gives, or stop to question the absolute rectitude of the adult thought and vision which is forced on the child. No wonder modern parents feel nervous about the 'education' of their precious children. The wholesale destruction of their new and wonderful vision of the world, which is going to occur when they are subjected to school education, is something it hurts to think about. Now Pat looks at the sky and thinks it might break and fall down because there are cracks in the clouds; now Mike says that when it is night the darkness creeps out of the walls. They call flowers 'smuffers' and motor bicycles 'Moka-turkeys'.

Very cautiously, the parents of any decent humility will tell their children the accepted names and adult ways of regarding these things, but always as alternatives to their own: not seeking to 'correct' a vision of the world as it is seen by new eyes. When Mike dreams, and sees his father and mother in his dream, he wonders why they don't know all about it, since he saw them there. Ultimately they understand it no more than he does, and if they are honest they will tell him so. Half unconsciously they will try to warn their children against the adult conceit of knowledge. They will tell them fairy stories, but always with the qualification that they are 'pretend' stories, made up by adults who would like to be children again but don't know how. They will tell them of things that other people believe but they don't, with that reservation. They are careful because their children are few and precious, and they do not want to spoil something that is as yet honest and new; but they know that once their children are at school all that inner life they have at least tried not to spoil is going to be violated with the utmost callousness. They are going to find their children writing and getting good marks for 'dreams' as common-place and untrue as the collection in Dr Kimmins' book.

These essays have not caught much of children's dreams – rather what children are led to believe dreams ought to be – but they are one and all revealing of the influences playing on the children. The book shows the process of education, especially of young children at LCC schools as the betrayal of a human trust. The free association of imagery which occurs in the dream, and everything else that is spontaneous, is blotted out. The children's imagination is not of reality, they never invent or make new words, and they have been taught to think of the war, in which their brothers and fathers are suffering, in terms of cartoons and of single-handed combats with the Kaiser and Little Willie. They have been allowed to prefix the words 'The other night I dreamed that …' to any favourite little bit of composition, and to get away with it as a description of a dream.

Even Dr Kimmins himself admits that the 'dreams' of children from reform schools are superior to those of children undergoing the normal LCC education.

By way of interpretation Dr Kimmins borrows an idea or two from Freud and talks about wish fulfilment on every other page. He entirely misses the point that the fear dreams of children are often derived from fear of impermanence and changeability in the external world. The fear that chairs may turn into living things and darkness itself breeds intruders. The children are stuffed with cartoon distortions and fairy tales, and it does not seem to have occurred to Dr Kimmins that one valid function of education for the very young lies in reassurance that the external world has not been found to indulge in tricks of unnatural metamorphosis. In the end we are told that children's dreams are of 'educational value', meaning that when a child dreams longingly of plum puddings and mince tarts, it probably isn't getting enough to eat. When teacher knows that she is able to regret it. And when the child is honest enough to confess to dreams which have anything whatever in them of dream irrationality, then it can be labelled 'neurotic' and treated, presumably, as a mental defective. On the evidence of this book teachers and school inspectors should be absolutely prohibited from making any blundering attempts to probe children's dreams. That part of the child's life might at least be left alone.

A very different book on child-observation is Mrs Thorburn's *Child at play*. In this the conditions of the experiment are frankly stated and intelligently taken into account. Mrs Thorburn sat on her chair in the room or garden where her little girl aged three, was playing, and just wrote down everything the child did or said, in detail, as it happened. The child was given to understand that this documentation of her play was her mother's shopping list, and the course of the play was remarkably little influenced by the presence of the recording observer. The child was microscopically observed for two periods of half an hour during each week for three months, beginning at the age of three years and two months. And she was also observed in a more general way from birth to the age of four. The record, which is set down in a truthful, cool and unsentimental style, makes a book *par excellence* for these people who have just decided that they can afford a child, and who desire to anticipate what it may be like. A fair account of how a human child does develop during the first four years of its life should make pleasanter reading than the awful stuff about pre-natal growth with which many modern parents entertain themselves during the anxious time of the first pregnancy. The book deserves a place in every mother-craft library. But those who have got over the first delighted gazings of parenthood will find that what comes through this book is not so much the personality of the child, as the grave and sincere spirituality of the mother, so strangely putting herself at a remove from her baby of three to obtain accurate data of a child's development and play.

It is a little sad that children should have become such strangers to us that we go out of our way to observe them like rare acquisitions; and sadder still that, deceived by the illusions of objective education and psychology, we are mentally segregating them from ourselves.

New English Weekly, vol.12, no.7, 25 November 1937, pp.131–2

Hail!

The first thought of many, on receiving this first copy of the new *Adelphi* will be: 'How sad that our old friend is now so slim, coming to us so humbly as a subscription magazine.' There will be many a sigh that *The Adelphi*, with its unique tradition, its steadfast insistence on the real in human values, its pages always open for that writing-from-experience which touches the essential in life, from whomsoever it might come, the magazine which has inspired so many of us, and become a little core of frank-ness and honesty in a world of lies, should now be reduced. For reduced it is.

But *The Adelphi* now comes to us from the Adelphi Centre. All that *The Adelphi* ever stood for goes on, but in a world of change, the spirit behind *The Adelphi* has moved into a new field of action. The change is partly enforced by and in much greater part a percep-tive submission to the need and circumstances of the time.

What is this Adelphi Centre? Well, I went there, as one of you from Birmingham or you from the coalfields of Wales, a reader of *The Adelphi* from the beginning, to see what it was all about. I found at Langham a big house, with beautiful 'grounds', once the country residence of a rich man. But the servants' quarters were no more, no more the distinc-tion between the front and the back stairs; what had once existed for the private enjoy-ment of one man had been taken and opened up for the use and enjoyment of many. Significant?

I found at the Centre good, plain food, which I helped to cook, and a 'warm bed nights' that it certainly did not take me very many minutes to make. I found pleasant and sociable work awaiting me, in my share of the co-operative running of the place, and, intellectually, plenty to grapple with, in the lectures and discussions of the Summer School. My stay cost me very little, and later, when I went with my family for a spell, the cost of living was less than at home. The cost of living was less than in this cramped and secluded cell in a waste of bricks and mortar which we have to call our home. The domestic things at the Centre, the cooking stoves, the tables and chairs, the pots and the cutlery, were better, more simple, and more easy to work with than we in our private housekeeping have ever been able to arrange or afford. Significant again? Yes, perhaps you will think it is.

Then I walked in the garden and found there that apple tree. The apple tree whose bloom and whose gracious carriage of branches has been there behind the pages of *The Adelphi* since it began, way back in 1923. You remember? It is the symbol and the mark of *The Adelphi*, that apple tree; the apple tree that demands freedom for its growth, that grows so well on our English soil, that blooms in the spring with such breath-taking loveliness, but purposefully, that later it may bear fruit.

But at the Centre, you ask, what was *going on*, what *is* going on? By lectures and debates, by discussion organized and unorganized, the examination of social theory, the interpretation of happenings in the real body politic in the world to-day, the quest for the truth in this field and for the kind of formulation of it which can move individuals to a new spiritual position. About Socialism, about Communism, Pacifism, Capitalism, yes, but something more than the mere reshuffling of the jargon of Socialist theory. The tags used, because for some they are terms of reference, but the search always into the contents of these parcels, not the tags. The real striving towards a communality in life, towards an era of production for use and not for profit.

But it was, in the main, outside the lecture room that I found that contact with 'genuine' people and with what is spontaneous and vital in life, always associated in my mind with *The Adelphi*. At the Centre, when a man is washing knives or shredding beans, he puts off the frock-coat that all of us wear when we set ourselves to write, and if he speaks it is spontaneously. The barriers between writer and reader, lecturer and listener are down,

and it is then the best things are said. And in the evening, when those who have not gone down the road to the 'Shepherd and Dog' gather round the fire, there are conversations that for delicacy, gaiety, and *appui* make the best of written stories seem pale.

Those who have not heard such men as Murry and Max Plowman giving rein, with the help of everybody in the room, each according to his wit, to all that is happy and imaginative in themselves do not know what the Centre may be. A trifling occurrence – as a lucky throw in a game of darts – may set off a conversation that piles anecdote on metaphysic in a precarious scaffolding to the roof of the imagination. I do not say this is a recreation and a game, I say it is in part for its reflection of such qualities of mind that I have loved *The Adelphi*, and truth is not to be got with a bludgeon.

I am sad that *The Adelphi* is now so slim, and that for a time, and at this time, much that is not direct to its purpose must be crowded out. But now this magazine is ours, its readers' and its supporters', and we must make it what we want it to become. In the past *The Adelphi* has been subsidized by a rich man, out of unearned income. We, its readers, honour the man who for so long made its sixty-four pages possible, we say he put his money to good use, and perhaps we may pause to reflect whether the bringing about of Socialism is not a job for *all* classes, and not, as is so often said, for the working class alone. But now *The Adelphi*, like 'The Oaks', at Langham, has passed into our hands. We must use it, build it up, make it into what we want it to be. Comrades and fellow readers of the new *Adelphi*, the opportunity and the responsibility is ours.

The Adelphi (new series), vol. 13, no. 4, January 1937, pp. 196–8

Into open formation

Pacifists in this country today are more numerous than our Government would care to acknowledge. There are pacifists of religious conviction, who believe that to sanction the taking of human life in *any* cause would be to give the lie to the whole of their individual human existence. There *are* pacifists of political conviction, who believe that to fight on either side in a capitalist war is to fight on the wrong side. And there is that great majority who will resist all attempts at conscription, not from any conscious consideration of principle, but because the certainty of being maimed, poisoned, or blown to pieces runs counter to wholesomely strong instincts of self-preservation.

These last, the young men whom even the prospect of receiving 9.37 pence worth of food per day is not tempting to enlist in the Army, are the active front of the pacifist movement in this country at the present time. Religious and political convictions shift like sand after each tide of mass influence; any change in emotional or economic circumstance may disturb them profoundly: only amongst a numerically insignificant minority, do they remain constant as the years go on. But the instinct of a man to save his own life goes down to bedrock, and is finally honest, sane and wise.

The sentiments-current in society to which we pay lip service are so crass and perverted that to be a pacifist from simple instincts of self-preservation is regarded as shameful. So we notice that the politically effective pacifists at the present time are assembled under no banner. It would not be 'nice' to have for slogan, 'You go down with the ship, lads, we'll save our lives', though nothing could be more sensible and reasonable, when no one *need* go down with the ship. Those who are now refusing to enlist because they do not want to die are doing more than anybody else to check the drift to war. Let us notice that they are not doing this by uniting together but by acting each for himself in open formation.

What of the pacifists of religious and political conviction? In so far as their convictions are more than subconscious camouflage of an unmentionable but eminently sane desire to save themselves, they are not numerous, but they include the conscious, the thoughtful and the articulate. There is a tendency amongst responsible pacifists to confuse the power they have with political power and a wistful feeling that somehow it ought to be organized really on 'party' lines: that they should band together for mutual protection and to pursue a corporate policy. Even if such association were possible, *is* it the best way for pacifists to make the most of their opportunities?

Associations and societies can so easily be suppressed or swept to the Right or to the Left through internal dissension. And in all group-activities the damp of self-regarding religiosity so quickly sets in, paralysing all sense of function and practical drive. If pacifists drop their hankerings after association, break into open formation, and keep dispersed, *they cannot be suppressed*. Consider the hunger marchers from the North. If they made their way in ones and twos and threes to London nothing could prevent a multitude from arriving at the common destination. Let fifty of them move as a body under a conspicuous banner and they can be dispersed before they have gone a mile.

The absolute pacifist is a singular animal. He is opposed to all tyranny, bullying and coercion, physical or moral: he cannot with self-consistency preach or seek to impose his own beliefs as a doctrine upon others, he cannot play for power in a pacifist 'cause', he cannot set up a new anarchy in society. The professional pacifist stinks to Heaven. But for the absolute pacifist it is life itself that is absolute, and infinitely precious. He recoils with horror from the terrible enormity of terminating his own life or that of another man. Life continues under tyranny, but with death life is extinct. For the absolute pacifist, no political creed, neither the support nor the defeat of Fascism, Socialism, or the British Empire is worth a year of a man's life. All these things are nothing to the difference between being alive and being dead. In no cause will he sanction the taking of human life.

His philosophy is that of a few, it can never be a philosophy for all. It is an arbitrary stand, and the epithets 'cowardly', 'romantic.' 'idealistic', 'individualistic' and 'fanatical' may be flung at it in derision. But that is the absolute pacifist's stand, and as he believes so will he live.

What can be the function of a scattered sect of absolute pacifists working in society in open formation? They will refuse to bear arms, of course, and they will refuse to make munitions or to participate in any direct preparations for war, but what then? Essentially conservative at this time, the pacifist will work for the preservation of 'the elements of freedom and gratuity in life', spiritually he will seek to disperse the vapours of death which are intruding into life. Specifically, each within his own sphere of opportunity and influence he will use his wits to quench the scares and alarms, to defeat the cunning and insidious propaganda by which the Government of this country is seeking, and will seek to shame, intimidate and bribe men into forgetting the worth of their own lives. With the powerful weapons of reason and ridicule, by the example of his own actions, the pacifist can make it more difficult to stampede men into dying for a lie – any expedient lie. He can put on a brake: according to the force of his convictions and the extent of his ability it may be a feather on the wheel or a veritable hammer thrown into the gears. But be it much or little, it is all that the individual pacifist can do. By association with others he can do not more but less, for the opportunity of the pacifist is that by himself he may work with subtlety, unheralded by any label on his sleeve.

So soon as this country is involved in war a multitude will say: it matters not how this disaster was caused, nor why we are about to die – if we are prepared to lay down our lives, why should not you? That is the test every pacifist must be prepared to face, and for every brave and generous man it will be harder than to stand before a firing squad. Must not every pacifist move *now* into open formation and prepare to harden his heart?

The Adelphi (new series), vol.13, no.5, February 1937, pp.236–8

OHMS

Watching the progress of recruiting propaganda has a grim fascination for me; it is like watching the erection of the guillotine through the bars of a condemned cell. I am not particularly glad when the mechanician makes a bodge of fixing the blade, I am not sorry when he does his work neatly; but I would not miss a movement it makes, I cannot take away my eyes. It is now February, 1937, and I have been to see the first recruiting film of the year, *OHMS*, at the Tivoli. It is an extraordinarily bad film, so bad that no one need think it will encourage recruiting by gentle strokes of cinematographic art. There is neither art nor artfulness in it. Produced under the direction of some unimaginative brass-hat in the Army, played by people who are embarrassed by the drivel they have to say, it is both dramatically and photographically dull, and nothing but boredom will follow it as it tours the provinces. Consider the story.

An American racketeer suspected of murder steals the name and Canadian passport of the corpse, escapes to England, and, having to keep up his assumed identity, finds himself landed in the British Army. He has a little low comedy flirtation with the Sergeant-Major's daughter – in an arbour hung with artificial roses; he is overtaken by the cabaret dancer who was introduced to get a little leg-stuff into the opening scene; he refuses her wanton embraces; she threatens to expose him; he deserts from the Army, stows away on a boat which he believes is going to South America; he wakes up on the troop-ship which is taking his own regiment to China. He is reabsorbed after a spell of mild disciplinary detention, and so kindly treated that he resolves to make good in this 'man's army'; he arrives in China (studio set, Wessex and a bit of Hong Kong newsreel) and goes forth with his regiment to help the grateful Chinese Government suppress inland pirates. There is an engagement (demonstrating just how much life may be lost in attempting to cross a river at the one and only point where you know pirates are wait-ing for you). He swims the river, ambushes a pirate, and gallops in his clothes to the British Embassy, up country. He organises the civilian cowards he finds there to protect themselves against advancing hordes of pirates, holds the fort until the decimated regiment arrives. and is wounded, it is to be feared, mortally. The heroine, who is there for no understand-able reason, puts his head in her lap and mops his damp brow while he makes a speech about having made good; he dies or just goes, and she gets the inevitable other fellow. That is the story. It must be very nearly the feeblest and the silliest story ever set to celluloid.

But superimposed upon it is some even worse documentary stuff, endless marches-past under dull skies, and fashion-plate parades of the smart policeman's uniform which it is now presumably going to be the privilege of the British 'defence servant' to wear when he is off duty. But the incredible stupidity is in the portrayal of the officers of the British Army; even I am unable to believe they can be quite so boozy, bumptious and criminally unintel-ligent as they are depicted in this film. Sassoon could not equal such caricature, and the public will not miss the point that it is to such men that recruits are being asked to entrust their lives. If that is the way British officers organize the simple manoeuvre of crossing a river, with the enemy at one known point and nowhere else, and with fully mechanized and efficient pontoons at their command, then God help Bobby Atkins, or whatever his name is going to be in this 'man's army'.

Any firm of toothpaste manufacturers could command better technique in film publicity than this inspired effort for the British Army. But it must be acknowledged that even competent publicity agents cannot build bricks without straw (or they wouldn't have been able to do so in the time of Moses). One would suppose that the idea behind this film was to show the Army in a new and alluring light: to draw attention to the rewards and advan-tages now offered to those who are asked to risk their lives for 'the Defence of the British Empire'. By the evidence of this film what

do the new lures amount to? The privilege of wearing a policeman's uniform when off duty? The humbug of that will certainly be apparent to every working man; not only will he laugh, as everybody must do, at this attempt to disguise an army, but he knows how much a policeman gets paid, and he will be the first to notice that this pay is not being offered to him with the uniform. Let us consider a few figures:

	Pay per week		
	£	s.	d.
Metropolitan Police Constable on appointment	3	2	0
Recruit in the Army	0	14	0
Single unemployed man (Benefit)	0	17	0

In addition to his pay the recruit gets his clothing, his rent, and food, variously stated in the Press to cost from 5s. 6d. to 7s. 3½d. per week. The police constable gets his clothing, his rent, and a pension at half-pay (that is to say about £2 7s. 6d. per week) after twenty-five years' service. The private soldier who has served twenty-five years with the colours also gets a pension, but the amount is so small, or the prospect of living to receive it so remote, that it has not been thought worthwhile to mention it in Army Form no. B2557, the booklet about the Army, available from all Post Offices.

There are just two ways by which our Government, with the war psychosis only developed to its present feeble degree amongst the population of this country, can get recruits for the Army. One is to keep the Army the same and elevate the pay; the other is to keep the pay the same and elevate the Army. Both ways cut directly across the whole system of morality on which our industrial society is, in fact, based, and the efforts of the Govern-ment to get round the horns of this dilemma promise to be vastly, albeit tragically, amusing.

To raise the pay of the Army to some-thing approaching that of the police would shatter the sacred principle that purchasing power, above subsistence necessity, must only be distributed for productive, that is to say, profit-making, services, rendered. To maintain a numerically considerable section of society, unexploited for profit, at an economic level substantially above pauperism, in the Army or anywhere else, is one of the most direct economic approaches to Socialism. In peace-time an army is idle and of intimidational value only. To elevate the Army in the public esteem, without raising the pay, to make it a step up and not a step down for the caste and class-conscious men of this country to become common soldiers, demands the exploitation, not of the old kind of patriotism, which is ragged and threadbare, but of some form of *socialistic* idealism. It is very hard, and most unfortunate, but there's no other kind of idealism about, at the present time, which *can* be exploited.

The price for a large army in England today is social revolution. We may yawn through such films as *OHMS* with perfect tranquillity, for the price is not going to be paid.

The Adelphi (new series), vol.13, no.7,
April 1937, pp.308–10

In defence of Mr Baldwin

Sir,
I fail to understand how Mr Bechhofer Roberts could have written so solemnly about the recent abdication, in these columns. Surely *we* do not have to pretend to be taken in by a show that from first to last was staged for our benefit. Knowing, as we very well know, that all the moves and all the utterances were dictated by considerations of dramatic expediency and with no concern at all for the truth, surely we should review these State theatricals with a little more intelligence, not to say humanity.

When King George V died everybody wondered whether Prince Edward would take on the Throne, as it was generally thought that he did not want it. He did accede. Why? Surely because both Prince Edward himself and all those who were stage-managing the Monarchy perceived the real grief amongst the people at King George's death. Prince Edward could not have refused the Throne just then, it would have been considered in very bad taste. What happened? It was arranged that he should wait until a decent interval had lapsed after his father's death, but not so long that it interfered with the Coronation, and the abdication was staged halfway between the two events.

Then there had to be some dramatically adequate reason for the abdication. That a man of King Edward's intelligence, who knew all about the Throne, should renounce it, because he did not care for it, was not the sort of thing that could be put before the people. It would have cut across the whole convention of State Drama. The glittering marvel, magic, and pre-ciousness of the Throne had to be preserved. There had to be a reason that a sentimental people, conditioned by regular attendance at picture theatres, could accept. What better, what other reason but Love?

Here events helped, and King Edward, who had just as much savvy as you or I, and was vitally concerned in the success of the produc-tion, knew that he had only to go about often with someone whom the public fancy would seize upon at once as his lover, to start a fine volume of discussion and rumour. This happened, and the next move was to place an absolute ban on the publication of any of these rumours in the *English* Press. By lifting this ban, in the middle of the second act, and instructing all the newspapers to publish the rumours all at once a most dramatic situation was obtained just at the right moment.

Then King Edward was put on the stage, in the part of a youthful Monarch torn between Love and Duty. That the Lovers were both over forty did not matter, it never does matter on the stage. Mr Baldwin appeared as the heavy villain, and with proper delays and difficulties the play progressed and closed on the conventional happy ending.

The Throne was shown throughout as something even more wonderful than the popular idea of Love, and the epilogue, when the King came for the last time before the curtain and in a broken voice told how all was lost for Love was perfect theatre, and it touched the hearts of the people.

We shall never know the names of all those who co-operated in this excellent production, but we may at least admire the actors. Mr Baldwin as Prime Minister had a big part, he was admirably cast for it, and he played it magnificently. His rendering of the long speech in act three was perfect. Mr Bechhofer Roberts's attack on this actor, because his part was that of a heavy-handed humbug, is wholly childish and naïve. It is as bad as attacking the wolf in Little Red Riding Hood because he pretended to be a nice kind Grandmother. I am sorry to have to go for Mr Bechhofer Roberts, whose writings I usually admire, but on this occasion I am sure he will agree with me that he should have had more sense.

New English Weekly, vol.10, no.13, 7 January 1937, p. 260

The Coronation Mass-Observed

Review of: *May 12: Mass-Observation day survey* (Faber & Faber)

It is very easy to remind the mass-observers that observation is not enough. The unbiased mustering by observation and experiment of a mass of facts, related and unrelated, was advocated by Francis Bacon as a first step in the development of the sciences. But it is doubtful whether such a step ever has been taken in the development of any science. The scientific workers – or natural philosophers, as they were called until recently – have always been guided (or misguided) by hypotheses of one kind or another; and scientific method has developed, not by eliminating tentative explanations, theories and speculations, but by testing them in a special way. Observation *per se* will get nobody anywhere; there must be directive and speculative minds behind it. Nor is it always very satisfactory for the observation to be done by one set of people and the thinking by another. Not only is this very dull for the observers: it is necessary to think in order to observe. Observation and some measure of interpretation must go together.

It is equally easy to remind the mass-observers that the practice of observing other people is not exactly new. Actors, novelists and dramatists all specialize in it, and they succeed best in making something of their observations and communicating them to others when they manage to produce good plays or good novels, which demand form, purposefulness and imagination, no less than observation. There are ways of making apparently objective accounts of observations express subjective thoughts and feelings. This is one of the highest departments of art, but if the observations are supposed to be scientific observations it is a form of cheating.

The promoters of mass-observation know these things as well as we do and their unbalanced stress on 'observation' and hopeful air of anthropological researchiness covers the facts that they don't yet quite know what they are trying to do and their activity has not yet any theoretical basis worth discussing. It would be surprising if it had, in so very short a time. They have hold of a vague but promising idea and are groping with it. If, by the co-operation of their editors, questionnaire writers, and plain-speaking note-takers in all walks of life, they can bring to light something reliable about the real living conditions in this country, and about the real needs, desires and feelings of the people, they will achieve something that demands our enthusiastic support. The news in the newspapers and newsreels is not news of the people. It is news for the consumption of the people, news of the ruling classes, news of political and other opinion for assimilation by the people, news of war and crime and vice, news of rackets and stunts and habits and commodities that somebody or other is trying to sell to the people, all mixed up with the jam of a little entertainment. It is rarely news of how the people live. The voluntary reporters of the mass-observation movement have to serve no master but their own conscience, they can speak for a vast unheard population. Let us hope that the organizers of the movement will take it dead seriously, and resist the temptation to make of it yet another superior game for the intelligentsia.

The first substantial piece of work by the mass-observers is their account of the Coronation. Some two hundred people, members of the general public, took notes of what they saw and heard on Coronation day. These notes, or reports, appear to have been treated as though they were so many film 'shots', to be put together by a process of cutting, editing and effective juxtaposition, in short, by a process of *montage*. Whether this process is scientific or artistic, and to what extent the personal tastes and convictions of the *monteur* can influence the total effect of the composite work – these are questions for consideration. But in this case,

at any rate, the film technique has been applied very successfully, and it has produced what is probably the best book so far about the Coronation. It provides a fair account of the happenings in the streets of London and about the country on Coronation day, not as they were supposed to have been, or as they were officially reported, but as they were seen by the general public.

Preceding the assembled accounts of what actually happened is a well-selected sequence of cuttings from the newspapers, revealing the way in which the forthcoming event was drummed up and invested, in anticipation, with inexpressible magic and glory. The official view of the 'rejoicings', the decorations and the crowds, was that they represented a great outburst of spontaneous joy and loyalty throughout the united family of the Empire. This survey examines how much they cost, who paid for them, and the methods adopted in arranging public rejoicings from above. The reports of the observers show what this elaborate and costly working-up of the public really succeeded in doing. Individual reactions varied from almost total indifference to qualified expression of the official sentiments.

No general conclusion is drawn from the mass of observations, but it appears that the most conspicuous result of the preparations was that about one per cent of the population indulged in orgiastic behaviour on May 12, 1937. There is something 'not quite nice' in this detailed account of the orgies (or the orgasm) after it is all over. The drunken roistering, the hundreds of tons of muck in the streets, the profiteering, the cheers for the men who swept up after the horses, the old ladies sitting in the gutter all night, the tawdry favours, the mauling of girls, the rain, the casualties and the temporary lavatories. It doesn't make a very pretty picture, the attempt to make up with the Circus what is lacking in Bread. Not when the Circus is over.

One matter which would have been of much human interest is not revealed in this survey. That is, how the Abdication affected the reception of the Coronation by the public. To have shown that would have meant reporting what the people of this country were thinking and saying to each other on the subject. Since only thoughts and sayings that happened to conform with the official story can now be given currency, the editors of this Survey are not to blame. But because of this suppression the Survey lacks something vital in historical accuracy, and the mass-observation fails to be scientific. There can be no science where significant facts have to be suppressed.

New English Weekly, 30 December 1937, pp. 231–2

The ten commandments

In the thirty-sixth year of my life, I find myself pausing sometimes to take stock. Of many things I am taking stock. And, by chance, in reading the Book of Exodus again for tales to tell my children, I have come upon the Ten Commandments. The ten principles of grace that Moses brought out of Egypt, defined in his solitude upon Mount Sinai, and delivered as the words of God, on a thundery day, to the wandering tribes of Israel. I am astonished to find in these ancient principles of Moses so much that I, of another race, and of another time, can recognise as my own. Though I have scarcely given the Ten Commandments a thought in twenty years, it is nevertheless true that as I have lived so I have obeyed them.

> *I am the Lord thy God, which brought thee …*
> *out of the house of bondage.*

The bondage that I have known is enforced acquiescence in the purposes and the will of others. I have perforce served such alien purposes, but I have never been wholly in bondage, and in so far as I am free, it is the Lord my God within me, and none other, that has freed me.

> *Thou shalt have none other Gods before me.*

And I will not. I will not have Christ; I will by no means have the God of Abraham or of Moses; I will not have the State, or my King and Country; I will not have Expediency and Convenience; and I will not have Mammon. I will not have your God, nor *yours*, I will put no other God before my own. Whenever I have sinned in this I have wasted myself in confusion. The Lord my God is a jealous God.

> *Thou shalt not make unto thee any graven*
> *image. … Thou shalt not bow down thyself*
> *to them, nor serve them. …*

I will not uncover my head before a cenotaph; I will not swear upon a Bible in courts of law; I will not kneel before any altar in the attitude of prayer, nor cross myself before a Crucifix; I will not raise my arm and shout 'Heil!' nor stand up when the band plays 'God Save the King'. Before idols that are manifest it is easy not to sin; it is harder not to bow down myself before systems of ideas and patterns of words set up in the likeness of what is in heaven and in the earth beneath. It is very hard to reject such graven imagery, and to look steadfastly upon the real, to distinguish it and to serve it. And yet harder to cast from me than the idolatry of ideas is the idolatry of incomprehensibility, of God the incomprehensible. I have sought, with uncertain strength, to stand apart from both greater and lesser idolatries, but in this I am weak and constant in sin, and for my failing my children will suffer until my part in them is diminished through their generations.

*Thou shalt not take the name of the Lord
    thy God in vain.*
The name of God is an image graven on the page, and this present vanity is sin. I am one who calls but rarely upon the name of God, for I have heard no man do so without falsity to himself. The Lord my God rests in a secret place, as it is my mortal soul so also it is my living quick, I do not know the God that is my Lord, only the inclinations that I seek to follow. I do not preen myself in the name of my God, nor invest it like a child in the image of man, when with my very eyes I seem to behold a world that is greater than man, and all the related life on this, the earth, of which man is but a part. The Church, which touched my forehead with the savage magic of its consecrated water, would have me call upon the Lord my God a thousand times a year, and the Church is damned in my sight. God is that within reality for which there are no words: I will not bow down to words and mistake my God.

*Remember the Sabbath Day, to keep
    it holy.*
In the plain tally of my life there has been one day in seven, and one year in seven, that I have sought to keep holy. On my Sabbath Days I have set myself apart from bondage and done no labour. But I have permitted no man to prescribe what for me should be holy, nor which should be my Sabbath Days. Those days have uplifted and blessed my life.

Honour thy father and thy mother.
Before my own children were about me I was without understanding of my father and my mother. This commandment my children have taught me: to honour my father and my mother as I would honour myself, for I am their child. Without such honour, and such understanding, my days could not be long in the land which the Lord my God hath given me, though I lived to a hundred in bondage.

Thou shalt do no murder.
By whatsoever name it may be called, I will do no murder. I will not do murder in the name of Law, nor of my Country, nor of God. I will not do murder for Democracy, for Peace, for Justice, or for the Defence of Women and Children or of my Heritage. I will not do murder for anybody or on the name of anything. I will not put out eyes that see as my own eyes see; nor spill blood that flows as my own. In this my strength must uphold my resolve. Whosoever may say I am an accessory to murder, I will do no murder. By contrivance and cunning I shall seek in time of War, to do no other than I have done in Peace. I will not bear upon my soul the sins of my neighbours. And as I will do no murder so I will guard my own life. I will not offer myself for a sacrifice upon any altar; I would not have my blood upon another's hands as I would not have his upon mine. With the judgment of a man, and the craft of a fox that is hunted on the plain, I will ever seek to preserve my life from peril, to live in honour and die in peace with my God.

Thou shalt not commit adultery.
I will not lie with the wife of another man, nor will I eat from his plate, nor utter his words from my mouth. I will not beget confusion. In fear of uncleanness and defilement I will not consort with the priestesses of the groves,

I will not forsake my children, but I will have no vows of fidelity put upon me that I have never made, and I will contract with no woman to be hers and hers only. I will put no woman before my God.

Thou shalt not steal.
I will steal neither as a common thief nor as the great thieves of the courts and the market-places. I will have nothing that is not mine according to the Laws of my neighbours; I will not hazard my liberty for chattels. But I will not lie down whilst anything that is justly mine is stolen from me. With slow patience and quick cunning I will have return from whomsoever seeks to steal my livelihood or the profit of my labour.

Thou shalt not bear false witness against thy neighbour.
There is no sterner and no wiser command-ment than this, and none so difficult of obser-vance. For falsehood is attested by silence, and if I would not bear false witness I must so often say my neighbour lies. His words are not according to his action, as mine are not according to mine. Evil foments and breeds amongst lies. With all that may ever be mine of truthfulness and understanding I can say only perchance it is for such and such a reason that my neighbour lies. My neighbour would have me repeat his words as my testimony, crying often that he who is not for him is his enemy. I would not live amongst enemies, as I would not be a hermit amongst my people. As I can know so little of my neighbour so there can be little truthfulness in my testimony about him or before him, and in the will only is this commandment possible of fulfilment.

Thou shalt not covet anything that is thy neighbour's.
I covet only my neighbour's contentment in the things that are his; but in my neighbour I see little contentment, and for all that I have coveted of others my sin is light. I covet joys denied me by my own idleness, but I covet no man his possessions, neither his oxen nor his asses, for mine are not the sins of a child. I sin in covetousness of power over my neighbour himself: power of influence in his counsels; and as I would have money, power, without thought or love, over his daily bread. But I have sought no more than the bread for mouths that I myself must feed; the uneaten bread which hardens into power has never yet been mine.

The Adelphi (new series), vol.14, no.9, June 1938, pp.282–5

On the Yorkshire Moors　　　Sept 1938.

I travel now as I have never travelled before: with the knowledge that if I choose this writing will be published. Perhaps that is a good thing to know, perhaps it is not, I am by no means cocksure. I have grown so used to talking to the air, or to myself, with the chance or the hope of publication safely distant, that I fear the nearer presence of the public may cramp my style. I shall begin 'communicating' if I am not very careful. I spoke to an experienced friend of mine about this the other day and he said 'God knows you for an amateur, but Fleet Street will call you a pro.' I do not much care what Fleet Street calls me, so long as it helps the sale of my novels, but I rather hope that 'God' will have no reason to change his mind. I have already typed out what I wrote on the Scilly Isles, and I have submitted it to my publishers, to the one of them who has the most pronounced liking for my work. That was last Monday, and while we chatted, an advance copy of Asleep in the Afternoon stood on the table between us. It was a new thing, and there was a birth-skin of transparent tissue paper round its binding of green and gold. Everyone has great hopes for a new thing, for a new book or a new-born child, before it has received its chastisement from the world. But we did not speak of that, we talked about the kind of book that these, very different writings would make. There was nothing ostrich-like about our conversation, we anticipated some of the least indulgent remarks that any reviewer could make: 'Mr. Large, emboldened by his recent success, now empties his waste-paper basket'. But my friend took the sample home with him to read, and the same evening rang me up to say 'Carryon', and he told me to buy another waste-paper basket, if that was the kind of stuff I was in the habit of putting in it. They were willing to buy the contents of those baskets. So it may be that even as soon as next year, these

Pages of typescript (254 × 202 mm) from the archive. The text breaks off at the end of the fourth page, with no continuation surviving.

digressive writings, this wind and wandering, may arise from the safe-
keeping and peaceful darkness of one of my drawers, and go forth in its
habit of gold and green. I am pleased at the thought, but I do not
swoon with pleasure. If Asleep in the Afternoon fails to make good, my
stock will be low with my publishers, and my wind and wandering will have
to wait for publication for a few more years. Already I am making the
mistake of mentally defending a kind of writing that needs no defence
and that is at its best in its helplessness. When I want to defend
myself I can always hide behind the characters in a novel, fortified on
every side within a wall that the not-too-perceptive call objectivity.
Mary smiles, as she leans back on the centre seat on the opposite side
of the carriage; this is _her_ holiday, we are going tramping on the moors.
She looks quizzically at my pencil and notebook, in action already,
before the train has started, and she leans over to dictate a sentence
or two that I might not have thought of by myself. 'With me,' she says,
'is my long hyphen suffering wife comma the woman thous gavest me stop.'

o   o

o

It is a dull August day, overcast and sultry, with threatening rain.
The electric lights are on, at noon, in St. Pancras station. The
station is dingy and dirty, and the attempts that have been made to clean
some of the grime off the glass roof make it look dingier still, for
sufficient light gets through to show up the murk. The twelve o'clock
train to Glasgow, via Carlisle, is crowded, and beyond the busy platforms
there is an unlovely view of a gas works. When we have left London
and its suburbs behind, we traverse pastures and arable land; but today
there is no light on the countryside. The trees and hedges are

everywhere a dark and sombre green, the fields are low and dull. It
is partly the wear of the summer, partly the smoke of industrial towns;
but mostly it is the greyness of the day, and the sad contrast with the
corn and flax fields of Brittany that I left radiant in the sunshine a
fortnight ago. We look out on a scene that seems to become in its
monotony, dirtier and dirtier, through a carriage window tawny with
unremoved deposits of smoke. London, Bedford, Leicester, Leeds.
There are houses of sooted stone and darkened trees, at the foot of
grey moors all along the Aire valley from Leeds to Hellifield. Only
the magentia of the willow herb, growing in railway cuttings and waste
places, and by the refuse heaps from collieries and steelworks, has
lent its little colour to this dull journey from London.

Up Ribblesdale, the industrial valley left behind, we slow down on
a long gradient; we are climbing between the moors. The sun is
struggling through the smoke-like grey haze. These are the Pennines.
The hills extend away on either side of the line, bare, grey-green in
the foreground, matt-grey in the distance. Not a house nor a road for
miles; no exposures of rock, only a close-shorn, grey-green waste of
smooth fells. But it is limestone country; the walls beside the
track are of limestone now, soft grey stone, and not sooted but washed
by mountain rainwater. The skin of grass and soil is thin over the
stone in some fields and the yellow ragwort is in bloom in coarse
pastures. We are the only passengers to get out at Kirby Stephen,
and we stand on the platform of the high station, looking about us at
the univiting wastes of the hills. It looks as though we could walk
all day, in any direction without changing the view. 'How would you
describe it?' asked Mary.

'As nowhere in particular on a Wednesday afternoon.'

o   o

o

But when we have gone a mile and a half down the road, and past an approach of commonplace modern houses, we come to the centre of a small, and old, agricultural town. There are a couple of hotels with AA or RAC signs, petrol pumps, and a cinema in a converted chapel; but many of the stone houses were built in the seventeenth century, and the deep-green and rich grass of the surrounding Westmoreland pastures penetrates the little town and flourishes round and between its stone walls, in the churchyard and beside the road. We begin badly, by staying at one of the AA or RAC hotels. The place is humble enough, with a well-scrubbed village taproom below and only half a dozen rooms, but the charge is seven and sixpence each for bed and breakfast. In justification of this extortionate price, there is a dining room above with the usual dimmed and smoky glories of mahogany furniture, and several pale and weary maids in the proper caps and aprons. In France one would not expect to pay more than one and sixpence a night to stay in such a place, but here it is one of the best hotels in the town. There is no evening meal: no pleasant bowl of potage paysan, with fish and entrecotes and cheeses to follow; there is no quick and smiling service, no open cider or wine. We sit and wait grimly three-quarters of an hour for fried fish and chips superimposed on the basic tea, for which the charge is three and sixpence each. We ask one of the maids a question about Keld, in Swaledale, ten miles away; she has never been there, she nevers gets out of the hotel except on one evening a week, when she goes to the pictures. The maids are really poor, overworked drones, shut up in a minor

The semantic discipline

Review of: Stuart Chase, *The tyranny of words*
(Meuthen)

The elegant word 'semantics' means, according to the Concise Oxford Dictionary, simply 'semasiology'. This has nothing to do with the history of the Jews, earthquakes, copulation, or the rites of Osiris. It is best to think of 'semaphore' and signalling with flags, for 'semantics' has to do with communications, it is a branch of philology concerned with meanings.

It is important to get this clear, for in his *The tyranny of words* Mr Stuart Chase warns us that we are going to hear a good deal about 'semantics' in the approaching future; and he puts forward a pretty fair case for what he calls 'the semantic discipline' in using and listening to words, as a possible way out of much prevailing confusion of thought and its attendant social and personal woe.

One of the most attractive parts of the semantic discipline is the deflation of all words and all statements the meaning of which cannot be established by reference to operations and events in the world of tangible things. Thus, all high-order abstractions, and words which are mere emotional noises, are to be replaced by semantic blanks or the word 'blab'. About half the present vocabulary of politicians, clerics, philosophers, economists and others afflicted with proselytising zeal will thus be swept away as so much meaningless noise. Absolutes will be removed from our language as they have been removed from the physicists' conception of the universe by the theory of relativity. And all such terms as 'God', 'Democracy', 'The Proletariat', 'Truth', 'Justice', 'The Logos', 'Communism', 'The Just Price', 'Fascism', 'Collective Security' and the like – terms as to the meaning of which there is and can be no possibility of common agreement amongst mankind, and which are, therefore, useless for purposes of communication – these will all uniformly be replaced by the word 'blab' and nothing else will become audible until somebody begins to talk about particular men and women, or identifiable group of men and women, and their bread and onions. To borrow an example from Mr Chase:

> The Aryan Fatherland, which has nursed the souls of heroes, calls upon you for the supreme sacrifice which you, in whom flows heroic blood, will not fail, and which will forever echo down the corridors of history.

> Would be translated:

> The blab blab, which has nursed the blabs of blabs, calls upon you for the blab blab which you, in whom flows blab blood, will not fail, and which will blab echo down the blabs of blab.

> … If, however, a political leader says:

> Every adult in the geographical area called Germany will receive not more than two loaves of bread per week for the next six months,

> there is little possibility of communication failure. There is not a blab in a carload of such talk.

In this, we can readily agree with Mr Chase, but he does not by any means single out Aryan blab; most of his horrible examples are drawn from much nearer home. The speeches of our own politicians lend themselves admirably to semantic deflation. Substitute the 'Mother Country' or the 'British Commonwealth of Nations' for the 'Aryan Fatherland' and you get exactly the same result.

As no reasonable person could be expected to risk his life in the defence (blab) of the great blab blab of our priceless blab; or to defeat the emotional-adjectival blab blab blab of any other blab, the adoption of the semantic discipline would seem very desirable in the cause of peace (blab of blab).

Naturally, in this business of replacing emotional and abstract terms by 'blabs' it is easy to go too far. Abstract terms are necessary for communication amongst all men of greater mental development than savages, but the abstract terms must have 'referents' in experience and observation; they must not be products of mere cerebration and fervour. They must be capable of definition in terms of the how, the when, and the where. For the ins and outs of all this, which Mr Chase makes entertaining, his book should be read. It is a sportive, and pleasantly light and jaunty treatment of a subject which has, it appears, received much heavier treatment by Count Alfred Korzybski in *Science and society* and by I. A. Richards in *The meaning of meaning*.

The danger of going too far with the 'blab' business is exemplified by my personal reaction to the title of this last named work. To me it just means 'The blab of blab', and semantic discipline or no semantic discipline it would take a lot of moral 'suasion' to make me read it. The book may be an excellent one, but the title puts me off. I am not at all sure that my native intelligence has not led me towards a better way of dealing with vague generalisations and abstract verbiage, than the semantic discipline. I tend not to read such stuff at all, and this, I cannot help feeling, is much better than wading through tiresome rubbish patiently replacing all the meaningless terms by 'blabs'. Certainly it is much less trouble. I have applied my technique with outstanding success to BBC talks and 'news.' By selling my wireless set I have not only raised the level of intellectual honesty and purity of speech in my home, but I have got a few pounds in cash, and shall save ten shillings a year on the licence.

But I do not share Mr Chase's conviction that the principal function of words is to convey meanings. He does not seem to realise that different sorts of people emit different sorts of blab and that therefore the study of blab is important in the diagnosis of personality. By their blab shall ye know them. My own technique here is never to listen to anybody's blab long enough to get tired, but to take samples of it by listening carefully for short periods. Then I go away and savour it in silence. I find this tells me much more about people than the cut of their clothes or the lines of their features, and blab-sampling is indeed one of my favourite recreations. I would not live in a world that had been semantically purged of blab.

Yesterday evening, for example, I bought a publication from a bookstall, which is blab from start to finish. It is called *Rising Tide* and it is full of photographs of young men and women with uplifted expressions and permanent smirks, who have got 'God Control' by 'having a quiet time' (with God) in much the same way as the British workman mikes off now and then for two puffs and a spit. I am grateful to the Oxford Group for 'God Control'. It must be very nearly the ultimate blank of all semantic blanks, but it makes me want to live. While the human menagerie contains hundreds of thousands of people ready to sop up 'God Control' and go about with uplifted expressions, I don't want to die. I ain't seen nothing yet. And when Sir Samuel Hoare talks about 'The Good Companionship of British Democracy' I can't help smiling inanely and feeling happy.

No! I am not going to subscribe to any movement for purging public utterances of semantic blanks. But there is one measure of reform I would propose. Experience is slowly teaching me that all utterances are really meaningless except in reference to the persons who make them. I used to imagine, for example, in looking through the pages of print in *The New English Weekly*, that all the different pieces in it were the product of some equal human mind, functioning in various repositories, but all contributing to one whole in some abstract and perfect world of mind and spirit. I no longer see it that way: when I happen to know the writer of a particular piece I say 'Oh, he's saying that, is he? Now that tells me a little more about him'. And when I don't know the writer, I at once begin to conjure up some imagination of what he must look like from the evidence of what he says; and I am more prone to guessing how he gets on with his wife than to weighing his words on fiscal reform in Transputamia, however important that topic may be. It all makes a microscopic addition to my minute understanding of the infinitely wonderful human race. But I protest that I get too little help. An article, or story, by an uncaught young man of twenty-five may be published next to the work of a comfortably prosperous, or much-married, man of forty, and these essential clues to the interpretation of the writing are not given.

For my part the adoption of a semantic discipline in the usage of words, *à la* Mr Chase, may remain a matter of personal taste. There will always be people who write decently and people who write badly. The latter will always predominate, and the letting loose of a new jargon about 'semantics' and 'referents' will never make blabbers write good English. The reform I propose is that every published bit, lick or morsel of writing should bear under it, in an appropriate code, the following essential information concerning its author: (a) Sex, (b) Age, (c) Annual income from all sources, (d) What sources, (e) Married or otherwise, (f) Weight in stones, and (g) height in inches. There is a lot of other information, of course, that I should like to have, but the provision of this simple data would do for a start. Given them, the worst blab would be of interest. If anybody wants to know what it matters about the weight of an author, I would explain that I've never yet met a fat man who talked like a thin one.

New English Weekly, vol.13, no.6,
19 May 1938, pp. 111–12

Easter, 1939. I feel that I have aged by many years since last summer, and indeed my hair which still looks dark in the mass is half of it quite white. The small flame of hope burns very low in me, and during these past months I have lived in a state of contrived anaesthesia, by deliberately refusing to think of the burden of the future, or of the ominous happenings in the world. My keenest pleasure has been in finding some scientific paper I wanted in this or that library, in usucessfully routing out some necessary bit of material for my book. Last autumn I was bruised by three things, the comparative failure of my second novel, the incessant worry over money and the 'Crisis', which for a while seemed to offer the same immediate chance of escape as suicide. Since then I have been oppressed with a consuming but wholly silent misery, relieved only by the intellectual satisfaction of teazing out the history of plant pathology. As I have withdrawn myself from what it sours my mouth to call a home, Mary has brought the whole of it under her influence. It is her place now, not mine. She has been working as a supply teacher, earning a little money, about a quarter of what we need, and looking after the house and the children at the same time. She has been tired, touchy : I have been silent, careful never to say anything that might upset her. It is just like living with my mother -- all tameness and politeness and best behaviour. Then to make things worse, Michael, down with asthma, has been lying on a couch bed in the back room most of the time. He shouts and whines and grizzles , and any word of rebuke sets him off into a nervous paroxgym which aggravates the asthma and leaves him gasping for breath all night.

At times when I am thus depressed and miserable, when all

Pages of typescript (261 × 204 mm) from the archive. The text breaks off at the end of the tenth page, with no continuation surviving.

endeavour appears frought with overwhelming difficulty, when my very
pen drags reluctantly over the paper, it seems to me that I have lived
all that worth living of live; but then, at these times, I never stop
to remember that in the past these depressions have always proved
temporary, I have come through them as through so many black fogs, they
have been succeeded by spells of good spirits, I have cheered up again.
When I am sunk in depression it always seems that I have gone down for
the third and last time and shall never rise up again -- that my utter
woefulness is final and absolute. But I deceive myself: there are
depths upon depths of wretchedness yet to plumb, immeasurably
protracted agonies yet to be endured before the nerve of life is killed
I don't suppose I have yet been anywhere near suicide. That is no
such sweet thing as it seems, it is any ugly wound, more near to
violence than sleep, and there is no certitude of rest when it is done.
No! I am not near to throwing myself under a train; but these spells
of depression are getting longer and more frequent. Will they run
together into permanent night? I do not know. It is hard to
remember over this gulf of time just how miserable I really was when I
was young; perhaps I have not really been so unhappy even during this
last year than I was when I was twenty one or two. But there is no
standard, no thermometer of misery; no doubt with the wear of the
years, my nerves or that part of my spirit responsive to mental
suffering, has simply worn down like the tops of my teeth, and now
there is only an ache where once was acute pain.

0   0
o

In the Green Dragon at Marlborough, a rambling old hotel, now cetering for cyclists and ramblers, the kindly proprietress has made us feel at home for our five shillings bed and breakfast. She has lighted a fire for us in a sitting room and piled it high with plenty of coal and left us to browse among a lot of old books, in worn calf bindings which belonged to an author of former times, one Merriman. There is a set of The Family Shakespeare, by Thomas Bowdler Esq., F.R.S. 5th edition, 1827. In this great work 'nothing is added to the original text, but those words and expressions are omitted which cannot with propriety be read aloud in a family'. In his preface to the 4th edition Mr. Bowdler expressed his satisfaction that his work had been commended by all those who had examined it -- and censored only by those who condemned every attempt at removing indecency from Shakespeare. He added that it would have given him a real pleasure if any judicious and intelligent reader had perused the work with the eye of rigid criticism and pointed out any improper words which were still to be found in it. But it seemed that nobody had been able to find anything left that was at all exceptionable, and he ventured to assure parents or gaurdians of youth that they might now venture to read The Family Shakespeare aloud in the mixed society of both sexes, sans peur and sans reproche.

How gratified Mr. Bowdler would be with the progress of his art could he be with us to go to the pictures or to listen to the wireless in 1939! Bowdler was a mere fumbling and timorous pioneer; he paused to consider 'whether the sense and meaning of the author were in any degree perverted or impaired by the erasures he had made', and he warned the reader at the start that the text had been purified, thus stimulating a very natural curiosity about the original. Nowadays very few fathers of families would dream of reading Shakespeare aloud at all, and everything that comes out of the mechanical mouths is thoroughly bowdlerised as a matter of course, without the least hint that the operation has been performed, so that there are few who know the difference, among writers, between a gelding and a stallion, or a eunoch and a man.

o   o
o

Savanake Forest.

'Members of the public, subject to express reservation
of every right of private ownership, are admitted to
the forest.'

But picnicers are not allowed, warning is given of danger from falling branches, and all who enter do so at their own risk. There is a gate of rusted iron, between two columns of decayed stone, as useless as the Marble Arch, for there is no hedge or wall on either side. Mary and I, thinking of this land of ours, our glorious heritage, pause to write down the hateful words of welcome on half a dozen notice boards before entering this forlorn park. Careful to respect every right of private ownership and not for one moment to trespass on somebody else's grass, we walk straight down the middle of a long, long decayed avenue of beech trees. The trees are very tall, leafless yet, and rather deathly, for the reason that every other one is dead. The rotten branches creak in the breeze and there are clumps of fungi on the diseased or dead trunks. If I were the owner of these trees I should not feel very proud to have to advertize the fact, for they have beentneded with no woodman's skill, but left to suffer generations of neglect. The gloomy avenue stretches on and on, it speaks of mortgage and decay, of the fall of some house of Usher. The lofty trunks of are greyed over with lichen, the moss creeps up them some feet from the ground. Above, there is a sort of plumbic blue in the clouds; it is a cold April day, with wind and a little rain. The black-and-white magpies swoop about. The rotten branches creak and creak above. After a mile or two along this sad avenue, we come to a cross road, with another eruption of warning notices. Presently we come upon the House, a low barracks full of private ghosts, with a wind-tattered flag on a pole above it, and the red blinds all three-parts drawn over the long gloomy windows. As we veer away apprehensive of trespassing upon some forbidden part of the decay, we reach another long straight drive, at the end of which stands a monument. Only then, with that vista and that monument, does the full deathliness of this park bear down upon us. We want only to get away, out on to some country raod, out into the world of the living, away from this private preserve of the living dead. There is a little coppice on our way to the lodge, with wire netting around it, and a tiny rabbit is running along the wire trying to get through. To my amazement Mary runs after the rabbit, saying that she will take it home for Pat. 'You fool,' I say, 'Come back. Leave it alone.' It is just what they are waiting for up in that House or in the Lodge. Immediately they would charge us with poaching drag us before Marlborough police court; or perhaps they would seek to make the charge one of common theft, for that would injure us the more. It would be their opportunity to discharge a little of that hate which is sour on their notice boards. Mary did not touch the rabbit, and we hurried out of 'Savanake Forest', noticing as we went that there was a grid by the gate, contrived so that any deer attempting to escape would surely break its legs. Oh, horrible, horrible, place.

Do not be lured by a name, gentle holiday-maker; keep away from

Savanake.   You will be prosecuted if you picnic on the grass; you may
be killed by the fall of a rotten bough, and if no other harm can be
done to you, you will be chilled and saddened. It is no forest, and
no pleasant place.   Try the open Wiltshire Downs, and leave Savanake
Park to whatever noble family it may belong to, leave them to taste in
empty solitude the last residuum of decay. There is a rot and a curse
upon the place.

o   o
o

One night last year I had a very horrible dream. I was lying in
my coffin at my graveside, but there was delay; I could not be
lowered and left in peace until the grave had been made big enough to
contain all my belongings, which had been brought in a pantechnicon
behind the hearse. For hour after hour the bother went on, the
undertaker wanted extra for the job, the gravediggers would have to be
paid overtime, the lessees of the cemetery had contracted only for a
grave so long and so wide, there was a lot of telephoning to solicitors
about the trespass into surrounding soil. I was to be laid at the
bottom of the grave, and then on top of me were to come my grand piano,
some two thousand books, all the old files of correspondence, my
snapshot albums, press cuttings, all my chemical apparatus down to the
last dirty bottle -- every scrap of the junk which I had accumulated
during my life.

At last the hole was nearly big enough, but, even so, the fuss
and the delay was not nearly over. There were a few things I had
forgotten; there came men with bills and women with tears to remind my
executors of them. I could do nothing to help, but all the worry was
mine. There was the little matter of providing for my children's
education until they were sixteen; something would have to be done
about the house. . . I could not escape so easily; there would be
no rest for me until all my obligations had been fulfilled, all my
responsibilities discharged. There was even the matter of reviewing
Eve's 'Life and Letters of Lord Rutherford, which I had promised to
review, but put off and off because such success stories always bored
me. Even that would first have to be done. Oh, and a thousand other
things, great and small: I had left so much unfinished, there could be

no rest for years and years.   Death was a disappointment and a sham.
All my life I had so ingenuously supposed that with death would come
release;   that beyond death was nothing, a blessed blank.   But Death,
no friend but a grim avenging spectre after all, said: Not so fast,
my friend.

The dream was horrible but now I am troubled by it no more.   On
the 3rd of September 1939 I made my will, and since then I have
discovered how happy is the state of having made a will.   No pantechnica
will now follow my hearse, I have taken leave of all the junk in time,
perhaps only just in time.   Of course it has meant more than merely
signing mybname to a document in the presence of two witnesses both
present at the same time.   It has meant resigning myself cheerfully to
the possible total loss of all my possessions today or tomorrow, and I
Have only managed to do it piece by piece.   I have gone round taking
leave;   of the piano first, saying I can spare that, for I no longer
want to sing.   And so to all my books, and the rest of the stuff.   Now
they may all be destroyed by aerial bombardment, or sold to pay taxes,
or appropriated by the Government, or looted by the enemy -- I do not
care.   In the end only these poor writings have been hard to
relinquish, the ashes of my experience, the record of my life.   While
I live I cannot take leave of them;   I know I should grieve for their
·loss, and so I am trying to save them: typing copies of the pencilled
screeds to distribute among those who have been my friends.   A few
reams of typescript, that would go in a suitcase -- I shall travel
light to the grave.

And just as this war has lifted from me the burden of my possession
so it has released me from all the longest of my obligations.   Marriage
is a three-party contract between a man, a woman and the State.   The

69

State has failed in its part, it has cast us into war, and as it will claim our children as it claims us, conscript for its industry or its armed forces, so it may for those children's maintenance and their education. Perhaps it is not so hard on the children as it seems, for they will never know what they might have been. Perhpaps they will be contented slaves; why should we teach them to swim against the stream, or to blood their heads against prison walls?

Paradoxically enough, now that freedom is denied me, and the State holds me at its beck and call; while I stand prepared to render unto Caesar that which is Caesar's, I am a freer man than I have ever been before. Now that it is idle to take thought for the morrow; now that I can commit myself to no plan or endeavour; now that all assumptions of individual responsibility are void and nugatory; now that I have only to do what I am told when I am told -- am I not set free to live in the present while it lasts? The wireless set on our mantelpiece informs us of many regulations, it filters many dutiful voices, but it only plays one tune: 'Nearer my God to thee'. I am a condemned man, constantly eating my last breakfast, or taking my last look round. Each day seems the more vivid because it may be my last.

You ask what there is new in that? Is it not a condition of life that death may strike at any time? May not any day be my last? You are right. The war has not altered this condition at all. It has only brought it home to me. Death may visit me any day in the guise o accident or disease or by my own hand. If I am shot or killed by a bomb I shall have been murdered, that is all. If death comes for me in that way rather than another, what difference does it make? I did not make the war, and I am powerless to stop it. War is external to

me as lightning in the sky. The State, in making war did not ask my
sanction or consent; I have no effective vote. Therefore the war
has nothing to do with me; it merely adds to an already long list of
contingent mortal accidents. But as it is made by the State it does
release me from many social obligations, it cancels the social contract
so far as I am concerned, and sets me free to live for the day.

Do you remember this spring? How glorious it was? I made the
most of every day and week of it. The grass hada brighter, fresher
green; the weeds in the hedges a new loveliness. I drew and spent
the last of my savings, so that I might live in the country, and go on
doing a little creative work while the chance remained : there was no
longer need to husband those savings for the future. It was but the
part of wisdom to convert that little money into the only remaining
safe investment: the purchase of a few pleasant memories. I went to
London to work for a week or two at Kew, and in the evening I walked
about the roads whistling ándt smiling at the house property which so
many hold dear. The rows of semi-detached houses — curious how men
would slave all their lives to pay off building society mortgages on
such property, and women would spend their time cleaning and polishing
the sticks and rags inside. One bomb and half a dozen of these
desirable residences would ~~crumble~~ become a heap of rubble; for all
the substance in them they might as well have been made of bamboo, as
in Japan. It would be so much easier to set them up again. I laughed
for I had already taken leave of my bit of property; the loss of it
would not trouble me.

It was safe to care only for short-lived things. For the marrow
plants with their yellow flowers in my monthly-rented garden in Devon.
They cost me only sixpence, their produce at the most would be worth

71

September 10th 1939

MEMORANDUM

THE ADVANCE OF THE FUNGI
(Defence of the Crops)
By E. C. Large

The failure of the potato crop in 1916, brought about no less by plant disease than by the unfavourable growing season, seriously reduced the nation's food supplies in the most critical period of the war. In 1916 also, the Black Stem Rust and other fungal diseases of cereals caused the loss of some four hundred million bushels of grain in Canada and the U. S. A., thereby perilously reducing the grain surplus available for the Allies. This loss from fungal disease in a single year in North America was twelve times greater than the gain from the whole of the ploughing-up campaign in Great Britain during the war. To look back farther into the past, it was a fungal disease of the potatoes, the Potato Blight, that brough Famine to the distressed population of Ireland in 1845. Again and again, when nations have been hard-beset, diseases of the crops have proved formidable and treacherous enemies, and every people committed to war must be on guard against them.

When the increase of home food production becomes a vital necessity it is more than ever important that available knowledge concerning plant diseases should be brought home by every possible means to farmers, allotment-holders and the general public. The yield of produce from a given area of land may be increased by well-advised cultivation, choice of varieties and the scientific use of fertilisers. But it is of no less importance that advantage should be taken of every practical measure known to science to reduce the losses caused by plant disease, which are often insidious and too little regarded. It is, for example, probably true to say that the average yield of potatoes per acre in Great Britain, could be increased by at least two tons an acre if available measures for the suppression of virus, fungal and bacterial disease were adopted throughout the country.

It was with such considerations in mind that in 1938 I decided to write THE ADVANCE OF THE FUNGI. For some ten years I had been engaged professionally on the technical development of new insecticides and fungicides, especially in attempts to reduce the amount of copper metal required for use in agriculture and to simplify spraying operations on the farm. I had made several inventions in this field, and seen them through their experimental stages to their adoption in practice. As manager, and later as consultant, to commercial firms manufacturing such products I had done much liaison work in the organisation and interpretation of field trials with farmers and workers at the Plant Pathological Research Stations in most of the countries of Europe, gaining thereby a good deal of first-hand knowledge of many of the principal diseases which affect the food crops.

My consulting work, since 1936 had not occupied my whole time, and I had written two works of fiction whose interest depended largely on

On 1 September 1939 Germany invaded Poland, and on 3 September Britain declared war on Germany. That is the context of this memo (254 × 202 mm), which must have been written to stave off any forced employment in the arms industry (see ECL's biographical note, p. 76). The preface to The advance of the fungi is dated 'September 1940' and by the end of that year the book was published.

the treatment of technical themes in a way that was at once realistic
and accurate but designed to touch the imagination of the man in the
street.   These books were well-received, one of them was chosen by
the Book Society, and in 1938 I had the opportunity of following a new
career, as a novelist, which was very attractive to me. In view of
successive 'crises' however, and strained international relations which
threatened to plunge this country once again into war I had to
consider what work of peace I could best do in the national interest.

It seemed to me that the most useful job I could possibly do,
utilisingbboth my specialised technical knowledge and such abilities as
I had as a writer, was to write a book on the defence of the crops
that might be read with enjoyment by members of the general public,
but that would be, from first to last, soundly informative, and
helpful to the Ministry of Agriculture in the campaign for increasing
food production.   My publishers, Messrs Jonathan Cape, supported me
in this project, and a contract for publication of the book for the
spring of 1940 was concluded between us.

The first consideration was how best to hold the interest of the
general reader in the subject matter. And I decided, I hope righly,
that by far the best way was to cast the book into the form of a
history of plant medicine -- or, rather, of the applied science of
plant pathology -- during the past hundred years. A history written
in a shrewdly informal style and as far as possible as a 'story'. By
this means the matter would unfold gradually and simply as it did, in
fact unfold, in the historical course of discovery. By going for my
material to the _original_ scientific papers, and news apers and journals
of the time at which they were written, I felt that I could recapture
something of the zest of original discovery, and present the essential
and useful information not to a mechanical plan, as in a text-book,
but in a form that would be moving and alive. It would be a story
very rich in human incident, having as its background something of the
general history of agriculture over the period, and throughout there
would be the fascination of following the search clue by clue into
the nature of the intrinsically intersting living organisms associated
with plant disease. Not only the fungi, but also, according to their
part, the insects, the bacteria, and the still mysterious filter-
passing viruses.

One other circumstance would assist me to carry the reader lighly
and easily to the understanding of principles which might be almost
completely incomprehensible to him as they are enunciated in text-books.
Everybody seems to enjoy reading stories about doctors, their lives
and work. There have been many good, and deservedly popular biographies
of workers who have made great contributions to medicine... but how
little is known of those other 'doctors' whose concern was for the
health of the crops. It is not commonly realised how much medicine
owes to those seeking into the causation of disease in plants, nor how
closely plant pathology and human pathology are inter-related. My
book, as it made its way through the grand controversies between the
naturalists of the past would engage the reader in the ever-interesting
philosophical problems of health and disease.

But above all, only a history could reveal the magnitude of the losses that have been caused by plant disease, their economic and social significance, and show in true succession epidemic after epidemic of disease sweeping the crops and calling into being a defensive application of pure science under stress of necessity. Only a history could show the available measures of defense for what they are -- not routine practices to be blindly followed, but victories of human wit and ingenuity. Only a history could what the present plant pathological services are, by consideration of how they came into being. Certainly it was not my purpose to compete with the many admirable bulletins, leaflets and other publications on plant diseases issued by the Ministry of Agriculture, but to show what lies behind them, and to draw attention to the information and assistance that is available, and where it is available.

The ADVANCE OF THE FUNGI wouldfail in its purpose if it did not appeal to the general public. Hence the choice of a title that might have appealed to Karel Capek for one of his fantasia; but that is at the same time aptly descriptive of the great apparent increase in the prevalence of fungal disease of the crops during the past hundred years. The title is organic and true to the spirit of the book. The only history of plant pathology at present available is Whetzel's short Outline which was published in 1918. Although invaluable, this outline was for specialists, it hardly touched the subject matter of the science, and it is already twenty years old. It has long been felt by the plant pathological workers that there should be a comprehensive history of the science as there are histories of medicine. It was not my intention, now was it within my powers, to provide such a comprehensive history of a vast subject, but as the whole of my matter is taken from the original papers, to which full references are given, the work is a substantial contribution to the historical literature. It is illustrated throughout with reproductions of the <u>original</u> figures, some of which are not very easily accessible.

The manuscript of the book is now practically finished, and though I have offered my services in the present emergency to the Ministry of Agriculture, I hope that I shall not be called upon until this piece of work is done. More than a years whole time work and most of my savings have gone into this book, which runs to six hundred pages. I have abstracted the material from some two thousnad of the original papers in English, French and German. The scientific libraries in London have given me every possible facility and help. I am especially indebted to the staff of the library of the Ministry of Agriculture, the Imperial Bureau of Mycology at Kew, the Science Museum Library, the British Museum, the Patent office, and the Chemical, Royal Horticultural and Linnean Societies.

m The detailed indication of chapter contents attached will show the scope and substance of the book as it has been worked out.

Opposite: In 1955 the thirteenth Duke of Bedford opened Woburn Abbey (the family house) to the public, rather than give it to the National Trust. The venture received much publicity. This documentation (329 × 204 mm) was presumably written around that time. It reminds us that ECL was a rambler.

For the Duke of Bedford, with unkind regards

W E L C O M E   T O   W O B U R N

CATTLE GRID

NO PARKING   DOGS MUST BE KEPT ON LEAD

TICKET HOLDERS ONLY

NOTICE: THIS IS   PEDESTRIANS MUST KEEP
PRIVATE PROPERTY   TO THE ROAD

CATTLE GRID

NO ADMITTANCE   NO ENTRY
AFTER 7 P.M.

PLEASE KEEP TO THE   FOLLOW THE ARROWS   NO ENTRY
ROADS AND FOOTPATHS

TICKET OFFICE   HORSE POND

ADMISSION   ADULTS 2/6.   CHILDREN 1/-

NO ADMISSION BEYOND THIS POINT WITHOUT TICKET

NO WAITING   NO WAITING   PRIVATE AREA   NO WAITING

PRIVATE AREA   NO RIGHT TURN

CARS AND CARAVANS PARKED   DOG'S CEMETERY
AT OWNERS RISK

ONE WAY TRAFFIC ONLY

LADIES   GENTLEMEN   DRINKING WATER

BEWARE OF THE DOGS

PETS CORNER ADMISSION 6d.   CREAM FROM OUR OWN FARM

A DRIVE IN THIS BEAUTIFUL PARK WILL MAKE YOUR VISIT A
MEMORABLE OCCASION 3/-

TOILETS   TOILETS
FLOWER SHOP   PICNICS
PETS CORNER   CHINESE DAIRY
CAR PARK   CHILDRENS' PLAYGROUND
BOATS   RESTAURANT
SATURDAYS & SUNDAYS   BUFFET AND MILK BAR
ONLY

FLOWER SHOP. AVOID DISAPPOINTMENT
YOU MAY PRUCHASE NOW AND COLLECT
LATER

NO PHOTOGRAPHY   NO SMOKING

MIND THE STEP

WAY OUT   NO RE-ADMISSION

PRIVATE AREA   PRIVATE AREA

BISONS   PRIVATE AREA   PRIVATE AREA

BIOGRAPHICAL NOTE

My concern with the fungi began when I was a schoolboy. I had an allotment on Barnes Common during the First World War. I wheeled home a whole couple of cwt. of potatoes one year when they were rationed and very scarce indeed. Reading some garbled account of Jensen's Heat Treatment in a newspaper, I boiled them all in the copper for a minute or so - to make them keep! Naturally the whole heap soon went mouldy and we lost the lot.

My next encounter with the fungi was when I was serving my apprenticeship with Gwynnes Pumps at Hammersmith and studying at Battersea Polytechnic for my degree in Engineering. We were then living at Richmond, and, for the sake of my health, I used to go for a long walk on Saturday afternoons across Richmond Park to the windmill on Wimbledon Common, treating myself to a cup of tea and a book by Robert Louis Stevenson at Wimbledon before my return to our home on Richmond Hill. On one of these afternoons I was struck by the profusion of bracket fungi on the rotting old trees in Richmond Park. I spread them on newspaper and tried to find out what they were from a second-hand copy of Berkeleys Cryptogamic Botany! I did not even identify the Razor Strop Fungus, the commonest polypore of them all.

Later, when I was living in a derelict oasthouse at Westerham in Kent, trying to write a novel about 'Metame' and me, Gladys and I were struck by the bad smell in Limpsfield Chart. We thought it was dead rabbits and it was not until 20 years later that we knew it to be that of the common Stinkhorn, Phallus impudicus.

A few years on when I was working as Engineer-in-charge of a little

/factory ....

This introductory note (254 × 202 mm) was written for ECL's illustrated guide to common British toadstools. The book was never published, although, as he writes, all the work of illustration and annotation had been done by then.

factory in Acton making and selling colloidal sulphur (Sulsol)
and the first concentrated colloidal Bordeaux mixture with the famous
colloid chemist Brother Savage and Emil Hatschek and Apha P. Wilson
as advisers, I got to know Potato Blight and Apple Scab very well
and was certainly familiar with the Honey Fungus, _Armillaria mellea._
By then my first essay, 'On watching an Onion', had been published by
Gerald Barry in the Week-End Review, I had my Associateship of the
Institute of Chemistry, other essays and verses of mine had been
published by Middleton Murray in the Adelphi and by Orage in the
Week-End Review, and I had met T. S. Elliot, George Orwell and Rayner
Heppenstall either at Orage's editorial half hours for tea in Chancery
Lane or at Murry's precious 'Universitas'.

In 1936, when the Board - Lord Kindersley, Hore-Belisha,
Major Thompson and other notables - had let their colloidal fungicides
business go bankrupt and thrown me and my infant family on the industrial
scrap-heap, I sat down, as a justifiably angry young man and wrote
'Sugar in the Air', transmuting the manufacture of colloidal fungicides
into that of making carbohydrates from water and carbon dioxide from the
chimneys of power stations by the application of solar energy, and
caricaturing some of the scientists and business it had been my lot to
encounter. Boots Pure Drug Company, 'Units Ltd.', in my book, acquired
Sulsol and Bouisol - 'Sunsap' in the book.

Jonathan Cape immediately accepted 'Sugar in the Air' on the
advice of Edward Garnet, and/was a Book Society Choice and a 'best seller'.
Cape threw a Cocktail Party for it at which I had the honour to meet
Rose Macaulay. Pamela Travers was also there, but I knew her, and she
had already given us a first edition of her 'Mary Poppins' for our

/children.

children. My Gladys ~~spent~~ got quite tipsy on passion fruit cocktails
and spent the evening in a corner letting two young poets tell her
about themselves. She knew quite a bit about poets and their poetry;
she took a Dip. Litt. in Anglo-Saxon under old Israel Gollancz.

In 1937 Cape published my second novel, "Asleep in the Afternoon",
which was about England on the eve of war. For technical theme I had
the invention by a little mathematician, Hugo Boom from Uganda, of a
tiny electrical device which he wore behind his ear to put himself to
sleep, so that he got away from the incessant gabbling of his wife,
Agatha. Agatha Boom was a loving and life-size caricature of Marie Stopes
who had given us a lecture on contraception at the Young Friend's Club
in St. Martin's Lane some time in the 'Twenties, selling her little
grey books by the door and bringing her beefy husband along with her to
show how good it was for him. She had threatened me with a libel action
in 1934 for beginning an article entitled "Children on the Mappin Terrace"
with the words: "Since Marie Stopes introduced Charing Cross Road to the
middle classes ...."

My next book was written to save my life. I was a pacifist and
determined to die rather than be conscripted to work on munitions which,
with my engineering and chemical qualifications, appeared to be my fate
in the impending War - unless I could somehow get a job in agriculture.
At first my book was to be a mere handbook for farmers and others on
potato spraying, but once I had started, like Topsy, it grew. I had
the mischievous idea that 'I'd show 'em'. Show the high and mighty
Professors of Plant Pathology that I, an insignificant novelist, could
tell the story of potato blight, the rusts and smuts of wheat, and,
indeed, the whole history of plant pathology a great deal better than

/could....

could they themselves. Ezra Pound, in lavender trousers, suede shoes
and pink socks, visited me at Wimbledon and wanted me to join him in
Italy. Sinclair Lewis sent me all his books and wanted me to join him
in California, but I resisted all temptations and went doggedly on for two
whole years collecting my information on index cards in the libraries of
the Herbarium at Kew, the British Museum, the Patents Office, the Natural
History Museum in South Kensington, and the Linnean, Royal Agricultural
and Horticultural Societies. On the outbreak of the war we bolted to
Exeter, and soon rented a little house in Pinhoe for £1. a week. Cape
helped me with an advance of £200. and I soon put together my book on
"The Fungi and Food Production". By a stroke of genius, at the last
moment I changed the title to the cryptic "The Advance of the Fungi" by
which the book has been known ever since.

In 1948 when I was working at Cambridge as assistant to Dillon Weston,
I had the temerity to go to Kew and consult A. E. W. Mason about the
identity of a certain pyrenomycete that had cropped up in my work. Mason
regarded me quizzically and hummed and ha'd and would not tell me what the
thing was until I had joined the British Mycological Society, for which
he there and then produced the application form.

I went to Muskets famous foray in Belfast that year. Hundreds of
toadstools were set out on paper plates in the workroom and the air
buzzed with all their Greco-Latin names for a week. Although John
Ramsbottom, Pearson and the others were infinitely patient in pointing
out diagnostic features, I learned to recognize only two species, the
red thread-like Fusarium that kills grass on golf courses, and the Piebald
Coprinus, Coprinus picaceus, but I started making engineering drawings of
toadstools on 8 x 5 inch index cards.

/Thereafter...

Thereafter we spent almost all our annual holidays on B.M.S. Forays. My labours in running a national Potato forecasting service were over by September, and the annual Forays in different parts of the country were vastly entertaining and enjoyable. The B.M.S. must be the friendliest Scientific Society on earth.

In my Presidential Address to the Society in 1960, I pointed out that it was all wrong that all our birds and wild flowers should have good English names while all but a very few of our toadstools had none. Mary English then convened a small committee to search the literature of the past for accepted common names, and, where necessary, to invent new ones. Elsie Wakefield, Derek Reed, Nancy Montgomery, Mary English, Parker-Rhodes and I laboured for several years on this committee, and our provisional English names for 215 of the commoner species was published in the Society's Newsletter in Autumn 1964.

I was encouraged by the appearance of 30 of my paintings in Findlay's 'Wayside and Woodland Fungi' in 1965, and I decided to devote the remaining years of my retirement to illustrating the rest of the species on the B.M.S. list. I was housebound most of the time, but my friends in the Society fed me with specimens as the ravens fed Elijah. Margaret Holden, who was then Foray Secretary and who also lives in Harpenden, brought in most of them to me, and checked the identity of them all, often with the help of Derek Reed at Kew. My long labour of love was virtually complete by Christmas 1972 when all the paintings were done and there remained only this Introduction and about 1,500 words of descriptive text to write.

E. C. LARGE.

Coprinus comatus
SHAGGY INK CAP

(126)
147

HINUDED

X¾

Amanita inaurata
7

TUNEMA

Two of the paintings made by ECL for his guide to British toadstools. These were all made on index cards (126 × 202 mm), and show his engineer's approach to drawing.

ECL's plan for the production of the final text of *Sugar in the air* (291 × 278 mm).
Such a plan is described in *Asleep in the afternoon*, chapter 22.

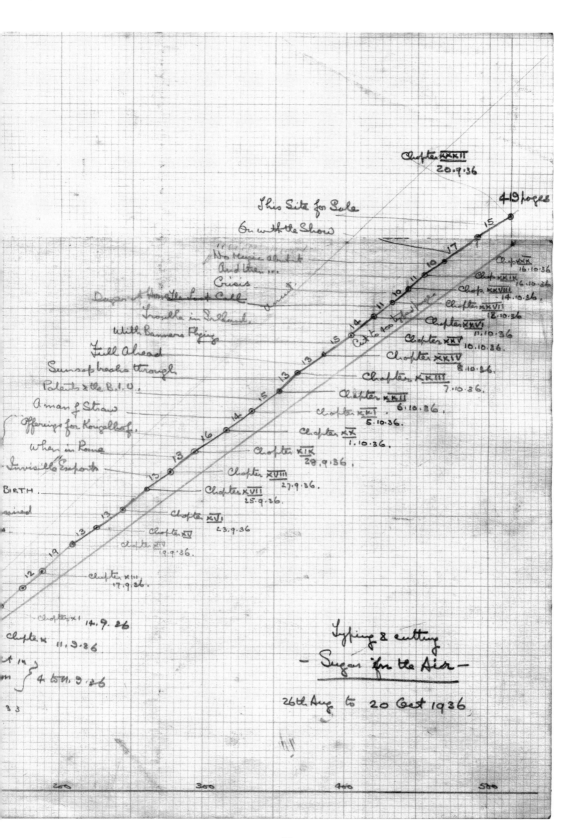

This Site for Sale

On with the Show

Chapter XXXII
20.9.36

49 pages

"No Magic about it
And then ...."

Crisis

Chapter XXX
16.10.36

Chapter XXIX
16.10.36

Chapter XXVIII
14.10.36

Days of the Last Call

Trouble in Ireland

Chapter XXVII
12.10.36

With Banners Flying

Chapter XXVI
11.10.36

Full Ahead

Chapter XXV
10.10.36

Sunset breaks through

Chapter XXIV
8.10.36

Patents & the B.I.U.

Chapter XXIII
7.10.36

A man of Straw

Chapter XXII
6.10.36

Offerings for Königshof.

Chapter XXI
5.10.36

When in Rome

Chapter XX
1.10.36

Invisible Exports

Chapter XIX
28.9.36.

BIRTH.

Chapter XVIII
27.9.36.

Chapter XVII
25.9.36.

Chapter XVI
23.9.36

Chapter XV
19.9.36.

Chapter XIV
17.9.36.

Chapter XI 14.9.36

Chapter X 11.9.36

4 to 11.9.36

33

Typing & cutting

— Sugar for the Air —

26th Aug to 20 Oct 1936.

Scientific method:

1 *Define the question*

2 *Gather information and resources*

3 *Form hypothesis*

4 *Perform experiment and collect data*

5 *Analyse data*

6 *Interpret data and draw conclusions that serve as a starting point for new hypotheses*

7 *Publish results*

ECL, 1956

Science, Fiction

Ideally this essay will be written with deceptive ease – or at least some-thing akin to the casual dedication in Large's second novel:

To E.H. over a bottle of wine

In other words it should embody the steady spirit of its subject, a writer who was always chasing the irreducible truth of each new situation. Both E.C. Large and his fictional double C.R. Pry are driven (not to say condemned) by a compulsion to identify local defects – 'What exactly is going on here?' – and the root causes are usually social rather than scientific. Such self-discipline is manifest in Large's ragged hand- and typewritten manuscripts, the understated precision and protracted pace of which are already lost to another generation. They are fossils of a practical decorum which has been abandoned, perhaps irretrievably, along with the wider implications of civility beyond language, by which I suppose I simply mean 'good manners'. They also convey a distinct sense of practice; that is, plainly *practising writing to get better at it* rather than some grander calling to *the practice of writing* – and in Large's case the proletarian overtones of 'writer' resonate more convincingly than the pretensions of 'author', as he implies himself:

> He set out the typewriter, the manuscript, the paper and his several mechanical aids to production, on his table, as though he were going to be timed for typewriting under the Bedaux system, but he did not yet start. Forty days and forty nights! Five hundred and sixty-one pages in that stack of manuscript four inches high … Even so, the typescript-production graph had still to be prepared. On this graph pages of typescript were to be plotted against the pages of manuscript. An ideal line on the graph showed how many pages of typescript there should be when he had reached any given page of the manuscript, if he was going to end up with exactly four hundred typed pages …

My copy of Large's fourth and final book *Dawn in Andromeda* arrived in the mail with an auspicious photograph glued to the inside of its cover: the writer apparently at work on the manuscript of the same book, sat behind a makeshift table at the end of a garden with a pile of what appear to be encyclopaedias or dictionaries. According to an obituary note the picture was probably taken on a Sunday morning, and this casual snap-shot of the weekend writer implies two ideas which are not necessarily contradictory – that for Large writing was a pleasant pastime, but also one urgent enough to occupy what was then still upheld as a traditional (i.e. religious) day of leisure. This is not lower-case work in the sense of labour, but capitalized Work in the sense of artistry; a *necessary hobby*, then, with as much allusion to compulsion, of being held in a grip, as to the fix of creation. The personal and communal dilemmas that arise from this conflict form the basis of Large's first two novels, *Sugar in the air* and *Asleep in the afternoon*, and given their largely autobiographical content it is clear that Large simply – constitutionally – *had to write*. This urgency, which only occasionally slides into desperation, is at the root of both novels' recurring motif: the struggle to 'win back' time from industry, the staking of a claim to *live* life rather than spend it occupied by the drudgery of labour, manual or otherwise. The elliptical fact that for Large this 'living' was practically synonymous with 'writing' (at least at the time these first books were written, as well as during the timeframe *within* the novels) is typical of the looping self-reflexivity that propels it.

Double bind

Sugar in the air is a story of the cycle of an idea. In this case the biological one compressed into its deadpan title – a novel's 'only line of poetry' according to Large (speaking in character). Charles Pry is a chemical engineer fast approaching the end of two years' self-imposed unemployment spent trying to write, who unwittingly finds himself directing an improbable attempt to produce glucose from carbon dioxide. To the surprise of all involved, not least himself, Pry's experiments succeed. He establishes a commercially viable factory, then involves himself in all aspects of its production, incrementally establishing the soundness and success of its product Sunsap, which is eventually processed into useful cattle feed. Pry then continues to manage the company long enough to observe – with public detachment and private dismay – its hapless board of directors dismantle the entire project. The decline is as rapid and reckless as its progress was slow and careful, a domino effect of conflicting vested interests in which the frequently infantile logic of industrial capitalism come across as both easily avoidable and depressingly inevitable. By the close of the novel both Pry's factory and his ambition have shut down, and he is precisely back where he began, having secured enough profit from the venture to support himself without work for a further couple of years.

Had Large stopped there he would have left a debut whose first impression as a rudimentary portrait of inter-war industrial relations reveals itself on closer inspection to be more concerned with scrutinizing the human ones underneath. Large carefully inscribed a double layer into the novel through a cast of caricatures (mad scientist, tyrannical director, jealous colleague, etc., with Pry playing the human being) who are at once *too blatantly* clichéd to come across as mere realism, and *too vividly* drawn from life to come across as mere parody. *Sugar in the air*'s default temper is sardonic and satirical, but both Large and Pry, author and protagonist, care too much *despite themselves* to come across as one-dimensionally bitter. Pry is more complex a character than the so-called angry young men who would soon populate postwar English fiction, being essentially an articulation of inward deliberation rather than outward bravado, marked by the constant struggle to identify, understand and come to terms with his own fundamentally contradictory impulses. This self-doubt is the core of Large's writing ('at its best in its helplessness', as he once reflected) and tragicomically manifest in the gap between his straightforward no-nonsense depiction of the anything-but-straightforward nonsense of human relations.

By similar oppositional design, Large painted his social backdrop deliberately larger than life, so conspicuously 'of its time' that the novel's more timeless aspects – its attitudes – are offset in greater relief. In other words, the false scenery is patently detachable (therefore transposable) and such technical doublethink is both central to the novel's effect and one of its key themes. Picking at the details of what Pry christens 'nominal democracy' – *everything done in the name of something else* – Large repeatedly attempts to reach beyond this surface to essence. In fact, this extract from one of his shorter journal pieces might easily double as blurb for *Sugar in the air*'s dust jacket:

> About Socialism, about Communism, Pacifism, Capitalism, yes,
> but something more than the mere reshuffling of the jargon of
> Socialist theory. The tags used, because for some they are terms
> of reference, but the search always into the contents of these
> parcels, not the tags.[1]

These contents are his characters' beliefs, conceits and motivations; *ways of thinking* articulated at the level of everyday interactions, not yet hardened enough to qualify as bona fide (theoretical, polemical) *philosophies*, and so more practicable: easy to relate, and to relate to.

But Large didn't stop there; instead he wrote a sequel, or a metasequel. Hardly pausing for breath and barely bothering to re-introduce the cast, *Asleep in the afternoon* picks up exactly where *Sugar in the air* left off, then proceeds to continue, duplicate, and mirror it all at once. As such, the sequel is also about the cycle of an idea, only this time a literary rather than scientific one. Instead of managing a factory, Pry writes a novel – also called *Asleep in the afternoon* – whose own progress is related through various summaries, paraphrases or entire chapters embedded in the outer story. *Asleep in the afternoon* quickly bifurcates into two stories, with Pry's 'real' experiences increasingly informing those of his characters – and ultimately, of course, a third once the reader realizes that Pry's writing *Asleep in the afternoon* is itself a more or less biographical account of Large's writing *Sugar in the air*.

Setting into motion another snake-eating-its-own-tail, Large concludes his second novel with Pry's first being published and acclaimed, along with enough advance royalties and promise of a literary career to avoid the permanent threat of a 'return to industry'. Both books follow an identical looping trajectory from a state of mental and physical inertia, through a period of passion, activity and enlightenment, then back to the former state, a sense of resignation and only the merest glimmer of satisfaction at having 'used' the time creatively. The books themselves – both fictional and actual – are now monuments to this oasis of economic 'freedom', two years frozen in abstract form of text-as-thought and physical form of book-as-object.

It is a platitude that debut novels frequently involve protagonists who are thinly-veiled versions of their authors, and one good reason for avoiding re-presentation of Large through narrative biography here is because the essential aspects of both stories are based on Large's own life, with little attempt to disguise it. Like Pry, Large worked as a chemical engineer (making Sulsol rather than Sunsap) before being able to support himself briefly as a writer, and likewise found himself at the end of both books faced with the tenuous promise of a literary career conditional on adequate sales.

Low modernism

My wish here is to insist that *Sugar in the air* and *Asleep in the afternoon* ought to be considered a single piece of work. To ignore one or the other is to miss much more than half the story, the depth of Large's art and the breadth of his work's inherent ambition.

With the slightest hint of derision Large opens *Sugar in the air* with Pry 'trying to write a book, a treatise', an introductory glimpse of the self-awareness that will intermittently descend into self-loathing. Here Large reflects his context not only by describing his surroundings, but by practising and – crucially – *observing the practice of practising* the self-consciousness typical of modernist literature of the surrounding decades. For years I've claimed that one reason for republishing Large is that his reflexivity was ahead of its time, but on reflection this claim doesn't actually hold up too well considering the lineage of involuted fiction that predates it. This stems from Sterne's *Tristram Shandy* (arguably further back to Rabelais or even Cervantes) then on to Joyce and Beckett, their German-writing contemporaries such as Musil and Walser, and later stretching on to writers as diverse Borges, Nabokov and Calvino. This branch of literary modernism ran roughly parallel to the 'heroic' phase of twentieth century art and architecture, similarly liberated by formal experiment and the exposure of underlying mechanics. Its proponents worked towards a literature founded on progressive realism (more simply – and problematically – under the banner of 'truth') as opposed to the supposedly stagnant presence of the bourgeois Romantic narrative.

The quality that sets Large's writing apart from these broad contemporaries, however, is essentially anti-literary: his novels (particularly) are grounded. While technically sophisticated, they don't seem to be. While the writing is consistently austere it remains generous, buoyed against its regular pockets of claustrophobia and desperation by a solemn kind of joy and stubborn, if still half-ashamed, independence. Take Pry's autobiographical vignette, delivered here to Sunsap's board of directors, who regard him almost fondly as an eccentric irritant:

> *'If you will consult your records you will find how long I have been with this company. Before that I was technical manager of a breakfast food company in Durham. My initials are C.R., I enjoy*

good health, I am punctual and industrious, and of temperate habits. I have no morals, no principles and no politics.'

Next to the show-offishness of the modernist canon (Joyce as stylistic virtuoso, Beckett as minimal extremist, Borges as vertiginous fantasist, Nabokov as shadow puppeteer, etc.) Large's debut novels are, then, unassuming. The tone, manner and trajectory of Large's narration is straight-faced, precise and plodding – qualities which might amount to a dour 'scientific' demeanour if not so regularly checked by self-deprecation and a tendency to daydream. In fact, Large writes with such alacrity that his approach might more accurately be considered 'low' in relation to the more cerebral, propulsive 'high' modernists, and suggests why his reputation fell quickly below the critical radar. Large shares something of the stereotypical British modesty and resolute smallness of such as G.K. Chesterton (astute observation and local pragmatism) or Henry Green (the mores of particular social pockets), but *Sugar in the air* and *Asleep in the afternoon* fall most comfortably in line with Robert Tressell's socialist tract-novel *The ragged trousered philanthropists* (1914), whose righteous everyman Frank Owen might be considered a blueprint of Pry in an age before irony, only a quarter of a century earlier.

While in retrospect Large's directness might be considered an alternative to – or relief from – the asceticism of higher-brow Continental modernism, the British critics of 1938 found *Asleep in the afternoon's* cleverness reprehensible, another characteristically British attitude which has since dogged a strain of self-reflexive British writers such as B.S. Johnson and Alasdair Gray. Johnson's *Albert Angelo* (1964) was the first of a sequence of what he called autobiographical novels, founded on the staunch precept that 'telling stories is telling lies' and whose narrative accordingly breaks down into an 'almighty apotheosis' of stark self-reflection. Although critical reception to Johnson's work was uneven (but by no means predominantly negative) to Johnson's mind he was always pejoratively labelled 'experimental', a term he came to categorically reject. Gray's compulsive Glaswegian oddyssey *Lanark* (1981), on the other hand, employs baroque appendages of self-parody (notes, asides, appendices and typographic play) which have been consistently read as a security device deliberately set to anticipate and defuse external criticism; a claim which grows increasingly vertiginous when some of the critics of this device also appear to have been invented by Gray himself.

The novels of Large, Johnson and Gray have little in common, either stylistically or thematically, yet it seems to me they have all ostensibly arrived at a similar point of artistic involution through serious, candid self-reflection. Their mutual commitment to an idea(l) of honesty – and the various formal solutions it has contrived – is rooted in a shared attempt at literary transparency whose intentions and implications are both personal and social.

This distinctly local breed of involution defines another overlooked piece of British reflexivity: Lindsay Anderson's feature film *O lucky man!*

(1973) is a three-hour anti-epic which follows its cartoonish naive-ideal-ist Michael Travis (played by Malcolm McDowell) around England, its scenes partly written in transit between shooting. In an extended closing sequence Travis, lost in an evening crowd at Oxford Circus, happens upon a sign – 'Try your luck!' – and is directed into an open film audition populated by the rest of the cast of the same film the viewer is just about to finish watching, as well as Anderson the director playing himself in charge of its casting. When Travis is pulled from the crowd for a screen test, Anderson closes in and repeatedly asks him to smile for the camera. He refuses a number of times, then – in an apparent epiphany – his confused, indignant frown starts to reverse and the cam-era cuts. The film effectively ends on this ambiguity I have since come to interpret as: *only laughter could steel him in his new awareness.*

Just as the art of Pry reflects the life of Large, and vice versa, this scene mirrors Malcolm McDowell's first actual audition for the director, which resulted in their earlier collaboration *If…* (to which *O lucky man!* can reasonably be considered a sequel). Anderson also worked in the same reflexive territory as a number of continental European counterparts, most obviously the French New Wave, yet – again like Large – departs from them where the work-turning-in-on-itself seems less the knowing gesture of an intellectual auteur invested in the history of cinema, and more an intuitive solution to a 'technical' problem encountered during the writing: how to offset a layer of mean-ing – the politics of transparency – drawn *from* the subject rather than applied *to* it.

During my most recent re-reading of Large's novels, I had the uncomfortable feeling that my attraction to all this arch self-awareness of such as Large's art was merely a matter of taste (like preferring red to green). This bothered me inasmuch as I had previously assumed the self-reflexivity carried some kind of critical, moral or ethical weight – a conviction which seemed suddenly groundless, or at best too oblique to be philosophically practicable. The more I considered it, the less I was able to hold the idea in focus, and it was some time before the itch was scratched by another anecdote to another introduction to another clas-sic work of involution, the extensively annotated version of Nabokov's *Lolita*, as compiled by Alfred Appel, Jr., worth quoting at length here:

> *One afternoon my wife and I built a puppet theatre. After propping the theatre on the top edge of the living room couch, I crouched down behind it and began manipulating the two hand puppets in the stage above me. The couch and the theatre's scenery provided good cover, enabling me to peer over the edge and watch the child-ren immediately become engrossed in the show, and then virtually mesmerized by my improvised little story that ended with a patient father spanking an impossible child. But the puppeteer, carried away by his story's violent climax, knocked over the entire theatre, which clattered onto the floor, collapsing in a heap of cardboard, wood and cloth – leaving me crouched, peeking out at the room, my head now visible over the couch's rim, my puppeted hands,*

with their naked wrists, poised in mid-air. For several moments my children remained in their open-mouthed trance, still in the story, staring at the space where the theatre had been, not seeing me at all. Then they did the kind of double-take that a comedian might take a lifetime to perfect, and began to laugh uncontrollably, in a way I had never seen before – and not so much at my clumsiness, which was nothing new, but rather at those moments of total involvement in a non-existent world, and at what its collapse implied to them about the authenticity of the larger world, and about their daily efforts to order it and their own fabricated illusions. They were laughing, too, over their sense of what the vigorous performance had meant to me; but they saw how easily they could be tricked and their trust belied, and the shrillness of their laughter finally suggested that they recognized the frightening implications of what had happened, and that only laughter could steel them in their new awareness.[2]

Experience and convenience

Reflection might be Large's (Pry's) defining quality, but his self-criticism is rarely wasted. Rather than wallow in his insight he *uses* it, as one critic noted: 'Mr Pry was quite a man, though I don't recall the author's saying so … He is no hero but he gets things done.' Pry's rite of passage through *Sugar in the air* is mirrored in a recurring conversation with his appointed mentor, Professor Zaareb, who repeatedly chastises his occasional egoistic preoccupations with short term success (generally comic lapses into vanity, materiality, or delusions of grandeur). Zaareb's mature, if not exactly zen, priorities are, by comparison, always 'for science', which is to say broad cultural progress and collective enlightenment rather than immediate local benefit and personal gain.

> *'You young men never see that Research is a cultural pursuit: you wouldn't expect Big Business to pay you for writing poems or having music lessons, would you?'*

At the beginning of their working relationship Pry interprets Zaareb's attitude as plain arrogance, but when he hesitates during the patenting – the public dispersion – of their research and Zaareb demands:

> *'You pretend to want to give your work to the world, don't you? Now that you are forced to do so, what cause have you to complain?'*

A humbled Pry replies:

> *'I am beginning to feel, Dr. Zaareb, that my real reward in all this is the privilege of association with people like you.'*

This exchange marks the end of Pry's professional adolescence – in part through the new realization that Zaareb's disinterest is a safety valve against hubris. And if this new realization of his work as a social rather than a personal project destroys some of its intense appeal (or 'love'), the same detachment insulates him against the destructive actions of the board of capitalists. As they plough through one slapstick decision after another, systematically unravelling the immediate practical results of Pry's two years' labour, his wider contribution to scientific knowledge remains immune.

Large's push towards a form of literary transparency can be read as a form of personal (and, crucially, personally-arrived-at) resistance to prevailing forms of government and other social management. That its righteous independence seems so pertinent seventy years on is a reflection of how the 'nominal democracy' Pry solemnly regards has only gained momentum since, towards a critical mass now defined (in modern Western society at least) by ubiquitous spin doctoring, the widespread distrust of government, and the resultant gulf between any state and the public it contrives to represent. In short, a collective resignation to the failure of democracy, or at (the very) least to lingering socialist notions of it.

At the turn of the century in his survey of *The Nineties* (2001) the cultural critic Michael Bracewell portrayed immediate history as a total inversion of Large's ideals. Contrary to Large's 1930s drive to get 'beyond surface to essence', Bracewell's 1990s stall at the subtitle: 'when surface was depth'. In this scenario culture has been reduced to a number of familiar codes: infantilism, chauvinism, retroactive reference and militantly manufactured 'authenticity' – all packaged through a 'comedy of recognition', contained by ubiquitous quotation marks at least a step removed from any founding 'reality'. This is the logical, tragic outcome of Large's 'nominal democracy', with experience supplanted *in the name of something else*: convenience.

'The end result of these ideas', Bracewell concludes, 'would be the feeling that, we, the consumer democracy, were in fact *post-political* – and afflicted with a Fear of Subjectivity'. The germ of this condition was already permeating *Asleep in the afternoon* some sixty years earlier – in the following passage, for example, where Pry gently mocks the 'convenience' of the book club which recommends his own novel as 'book of the month':

> *Wonderful! No routing about in second-hand book shops; no venturing and searching for themselves; no counting the money in their pockets before plunging on a book they had slowly come to desire. No carrying the coveted book home, under their coat, hiding it from Mary or saying it cost rather less than it did, half ashamed of the extravagance, when it could have been read for nothing, sooner or later, at the British Museum. No looking over their shelves and seeing how their taste and understanding had grown with the years. No sense that the choice of books was like the choice of friends. Perhaps they had their friends, and maybe also their*

> concubines, chosen for them by a selection committee. What a
> lot of trouble it saved.

Large repeatedly draws attention to this loss of experience in the face of convenience, and invokes the corollary 'convenience' of hollow political rhetoric versus the 'experience' of quantifiable and verifiable facts. His own prose is accordingly artless, stripped of affectation, its voice a familiar, even-tempered common denominator. The usually reticent Pry even finds himself heckling a speaker on the subject in *Asleep in the afternoon*:

> 'The contradiction to which the bourgeois speaker draws
> attention is dialectical and inevitable under capitalism.'
> There was a murmur of approval; the meeting seemed to
> find this answer completely satisfactory.
> 'That is so much cant,' said Pry, 'and one useful way of
> preserving culture is to speak plain English.'

Pry's call for common language here is supported by Large's example, writing the scene specifically and economically himself, casting out 'about half the present vocabulary of politicians, clerics, philosophers, economists and others afflicted with proselytising zeal'. In a contemporaneous book review (of *The tyranny of words*) for *The New English Weekly* he promotes such 'semantic discipline' by trawling various examples of overblown rhetoric and censoring each redundant word with a pragmatic 'blab' to emphasize the point.[3]

Classic Romantic

Large's writing is rife with multiple meanings, carefully crafted for the close reader whose assumed absence is but one aspect of his artistic melancholy: 'two or three people in a thousand would taste it, and it would warm the cockles of their crapulous hearts' acknowledges Pry with a kind of bitter, self-preserving glee when 'explaining' the poetry of *Asleep in the afternoon*'s title to Mary. 'All the rest might think it wholly sweet and delightful ...'. Large's chapter headings alone are rife with double and triple entendres, but the novels' shared subtitle, 'A Romance' is more prominent and allusive than most for a number of reasons.

First, because the tone and stance of both books are consistently – romantically – against all odds, their very publication barely believed by Large himself as some miracle combination of trial, error, good fortune and timing. Second, with regard to the fact that the definition of romance as '*ardent emotional attachment or involvement between two people*' could be rewritten as '*... between a person and his work*' to describe Large's (Pry's) professional temperament – or equally, '*... between an author and his reader*', for that matter. Third, because of the constant sense of his trespassing on a foreign discipline, romantically spending (or wasting) time and effort on an activity without immediate or obvious gain, and most regularly justified to himself as a debt owed in lieu of time lost to prolonged study and forced labour. Fourth, with regard to that essential uselessness of writing which affords it ironic agency, manipulating the ills of marriage, industry, government and religion into art – the romantic distillation of sugary life from dead air.

But above all because of the audacity with which Large slips his contrariness past the reader (on the title page!) by assuming the guise of conventional scene-characters-plot Romantic novels – which they *are*, in part; but they use rather than embody the form, and the distinction is critical. *Sugar in the air* is a straightforward indictment of industrial capitalism and its attendant envy, greed and avarice, while *Asleep in the afternoon* admonishes a public contentedly dormant on the eve of war. Ultimately, Pry (Large) is resigned to the deeper causes of both circumstances, and takes only the flimsiest, most suspicious comfort in the apparent dignity of his art as a personal stand (or coping device). Another critic portrayed him as being

> *so competent in his work and dedicated to it and personally decent, in short so expressive of the qualities we demand of any proper citizen, that he has no time or thought for self-advertising and thrusting and bald advancement and front, and is thus naturally put out like garbage in the end, the pure damn fool.*[4]

As an overview of Large's four published books, *Sugar in the air* (1937) is a piece of fiction about science, *Asleep in the afternoon* (1938) is fiction about the science of writing fiction, *The advance of the fungi* (1940) is a history of science with the tone of fiction, and *Dawn in Andromeda* (1957) is 'pure' science fiction (which is to say that for the first time it adheres to the conventions of a genre and is less inspired for doing so). Again, this cross-pollination of approaches, voices and genres from Large's various careers seems to be rooted in Large's autodidactic discipline, the constant flexing and toning of a literary muscle.

We leave Pry at the close of *Asleep in the afternoon*, his 'book of the month' a confirmed best-seller, considering a return to science and an adventure involving organic micro-cultures rather than London's literary culture. Having dutifully trawled his own reviews with amusement and breezily observed the dismantling of his book's window display, the folly of writing seems adequately drained from our anti-hero's system – he is suddenly prepared for a profession instead of a romance. And so Pry's circular existence starts over, once again mirroring Large's actual circumstances. The poor commercial and critical reception of *Asleep in the afternoon* appears to have extinguished the chance of his shorter non-fiction being published. In any case, the Second World War intervened, and Large's next major undertaking – analysis of a national potato blight – was to 'save his life': agricultural research was acceptable war work for a sworn Pacifist.

While it seems that, professionally at least, Large never really reconciled the division of his scientific and literary work, it is precisely the symbiosis of the two that animates his early fiction today. His writing is defined by a wide-ranging set of interests, temperament and capacity which is equal parts classic and romantic – a duality which extends to any of the parallel dichotomies itemized by Robert M. Pirsig in his *Zen and the art of motorcycle maintenance*: scientific vs. artistic, technical vs. human, or rational vs. emotional. Pirsig sets up these opposites in order to assert that the fundamental misunderstanding, disinformation, mistrust and hostility which characterizes modern societies are rooted in the personal and communal inability to reconcile these two poles:

> *Persons tend to think and feel exclusively in one mode or the other and in doing so tend to misunderstand and underestimate what the other mode is all about. But no one is willing to give up the truth as he sees it, and as far as I know, no one now living has any real reconciliation of these truths or modes. There is no point at which these visions of reality are unified.*[5]

Like the small number of writers who have informed the present essay,[6] Large's body of work is radical and instructive precisely because it covers all bases. His output ranges from the early reveries and reviews, through political commentary on topical issues (air raid shelters, conscription, propaganda), the domestic concerns of the family home and his 'wind and wandering' travelogues, through to later papers on plant pathology. Whether 'About the working class' or 'The control of potato blight', all are afforded the same serious consideration, dissected with impartial intellect, and the 'findings' articulated through the bricks-and-mortar construction of pragmatic argument.

*

The careful ceremony of dismantling and reassembling the typewriter; the graphs which variously chart the novels' progression and diminishing bank savings; the writer's block, analysed, diagnosed, treated and resolved within the space of a single chapter; and the vertiginous craft with which the wife's knowing-her-husband-better-than-he-knows-himself is captured by necessarily knowing *her* a step better yet in order to portray it – all are vignettes drawn simultaneously from Large's and Pry's life and fiction which describe the unique disposition of the scientist-writer. Yet none are quite as succinct as his anticipation of the deft Möbius Strip of *Asleep in the afternoon*'s design:

> *in a year I should pass through a rich variety of moods*

> ∴   *so would the book*

> ∴   *in that at least it would have some verisimilitude to life*

Stuart Bailey

Notes
1. 'Hail!'; see p.44 of this volume.
2. Alfred Appel, Jr., *The annotated Lolita* [revised edition, 1991], London: Penguin Books, 1995.
3. 'The semantic discipline'; see p.59 of this volume.
4. Otis Ferguson, 'One for the reader' (review of *Sugar in the air*), *The New Republic*, 8 September 1937, pp.139–40.
5. Robert M. Pirsig, *Zen and the art of motorcycle maintenance* [1974], New York: Bantam Books, 1981, p.62.
6. In particular, Large's approach falls in line with most of the other writers published by Hyphen Press. There are brief, enigmatic allusions to Large's novels in the books, notes and correspondence of Norman Potter and Anthony Froshaug, for example, which I like to imagine were deliberate acts of clue-planting for future close readers. Like Large, these writers work by simultaneous elucidation and example to articulate ideas which are the contents of the package represented by the label 'modernism'; contents implied by this last excerpt from *Sugar in the air* which refers to another fleeting critical spirit, the shadowy 'Muller', who – tellingly – disappears from the opening pages of the novel as soon as his point has been made:

> When Muller quietly demonstrated that there are no 'Laws' in nature, that 'Facts' are only notions widely accepted, and that the subject matters of religion and philosophy are things more real than concrete and chrome steel, Pry was greatly shocked and surprised. When Muller went on to the subject of 'Values' Pry found that those things which he had come to regard as his ideals were falling about his head in a litter of unimportance, and his whole attitude to 'Life' stood revealed to him as trumpery, adolescent and mean. For this he blamed his social environment – until Muller went on to talk about 'Environment'.